The UK SPA network: its scope and content

JOINT NATURE CONSERVATION COMMITTEE

The UK SPA network: its scope and content

Volume 1: Rationale for the selection of sites

Editors
D.A. Stroud, D. Chambers, S. Cook, N. Buxton, B. Fraser, P. Clement,
P. Lewis, I. McLean, H. Baker & S. Whitehead

with the assistance of
S. Brocklehurst, A.F. Brown, S. Buckton, N. Burton, N. Clark, C. Easton,
R. Johnston, C. Hall, N. Hodgetts, A. Law, J. Kirby, J. Miles, B. Miller,
M.A. Ogilvie, J. Robinson, H. Riley, T. Salmon, R. Saunders, A. Sim, P. Stuttard,
M.L. Tasker, R. West, R. Weyl, P. Whitfield, R. Woodburn & J. Young

Joint Nature Conservation Committee
Monkstone House
City Road
Peterborough
PE1 1JY
UK

ISBN 1 86107 529 4

Contents

Volume 2: Species Accounts

Volume 3: Site Accounts, Maps and Lists

Executive summary

- This report presents the UK network of Special Protection Areas (SPAs) identified to meet UK obligations under Article 4 of the European Union's Directive on the conservation of wild birds (EC/79/409 as modified) ('the Birds Directive').

- The SPA network presented in this report is the result of a review undertaken by the UK Joint Nature Conservation Committee together with the Environment and Heritage Service of Northern Ireland, the Countryside Council for Wales, Scottish Natural Heritage and English Nature. The network of sites has been formally recommended to government by the Joint Committee.

- Publication of this review has been guided by a Steering Group comprising representatives of the statutory conservation agencies as well as the National Assembly for Wales, the Scottish Executive and the Department of the Environment, Transport and the Regions.

- This review updates the assessment of UK SPAs published in 1992. Since that time, there has been a range of new ornithological surveys undertaken throughout the UK, especially in the uplands and related to a number of species that were highlighted as being poorly represented in the national network proposed in the early 1990s. In view of new information and possible gaps, Government requested JNCC to review the UK SPA network with a view to recommending a definitive list of sites, identified against explicit selection guidelines.

- JNCC has derived guidelines for selecting SPAs, building on existing UK and international practice and precedent. In the absence of agreed European guidelines, there may be scope for their use elsewhere.

- The guidelines have been used to assess the conservation requirements of species listed in Annex I of the Birds Directive and/or migratory species regularly occurring in the UK, and to identify an appropriate suite of SPAs for each species. For Annex I species, assessments have been made at either national scale (Great Britain) or, in the case of Northern Ireland, in an all-Ireland context. For migratory species not listed on Annex I, assessments have been made at an international scale (*i.e.* the relevant biogeographic or flyway populations).

- The SPA suites for each species collectively form the UK SPA network – a contribution to the European Union's Natura 2000 network – that comprises 243 sites. The network extends to c. 1,454,500 ha (see map below).

- Appendix 6 of this report presents accounts for 103 species for which SPAs have been selected. These accounts summarise the species' conservation requirements in the different seasons in which they are present in the UK. They also outline the reasoning underlying the selection of each species' SPA suite.

- Appendix 7 describes each site in the UK's SPA network in a standard format indicating for which species the site has been selected, the features that are important for these species, and the proportion of national or international populations supported.

- The review has been based on best-available data for sites and populations from the first half of the 1990s. The data were the most current and comprehensive that were available at the commencement of the review. They thus provide a comparative assessment for a limited period, and a fixed baseline, even though more recent data have since become available.

- The UK is of major international importance for several groups of birds. These include: breeding seabirds, wintering and passage wildfowl and waders, birds of Britain's distinctive uplands, and birds of the Caledonian pine-forest. A high proportion – in some cases all – of the national and international populations of such species utilise the UK SPA network. In summer, the network holds over 4,946,000 breeding seabirds, whilst in winter it supports an average of over 2,186,000 non-breeding waterbirds. The habitat protection provided for these birds is a major contribution to their international conservation.

● Those species of greatest conservation concern (in the context of the Birds Directive) tend to have the highest proportions of their populations within the UK SPA network, as do those that have the smallest geographic ranges (in summer and winter), and those where the UK holds a high proportion of international numbers.

● SPAs are inappropriate for some UK bird species and thus for these, SPAs have not been selected. This report documents those populations which are broadly and/or sparsely dispersed or where are other reasons why site-protection measures under the Birds Directive are inappropriate, this report documents these. The special protection measures for these species are instead provided by legal protection, together with a range of wider-countryside conservation policies and other initiatives.

● It has not been possible to identify a full SPA suite for a small number of species because of currently changing status or lack of data. Monitoring schemes are being developed to give feedback on changing population status of species within each SPA as well as at national level. This, together with an ever-increasing knowledge of conservation requirements, will allow the UK to modify the SPA network if essential.

● There are minor differences between the UK list of SPAs and BirdLife International's Important Bird Areas inventory. This is unsurprising – indeed, it is to be expected – since different selection guidelines, criteria, and priorities have been used to identify the respective site networks. The UK SPA list more accurately reflects the obligations under the Birds Directive.

● The carefully selected SPA network is of large size, contains a wide variety of habitats and includes sites spread throughout the UK. The network is logically and scientifically derived, collectively robust, and will make an enduring contribution to the conservation of Britain's birds.

● The SPA network presented here provides for the site-based requirements of Birds Directive Annex I and migratory species that regularly occur in the UK. It will enable the UK to meet fully its obligations under the Directive to conserve its internationally important bird fauna.

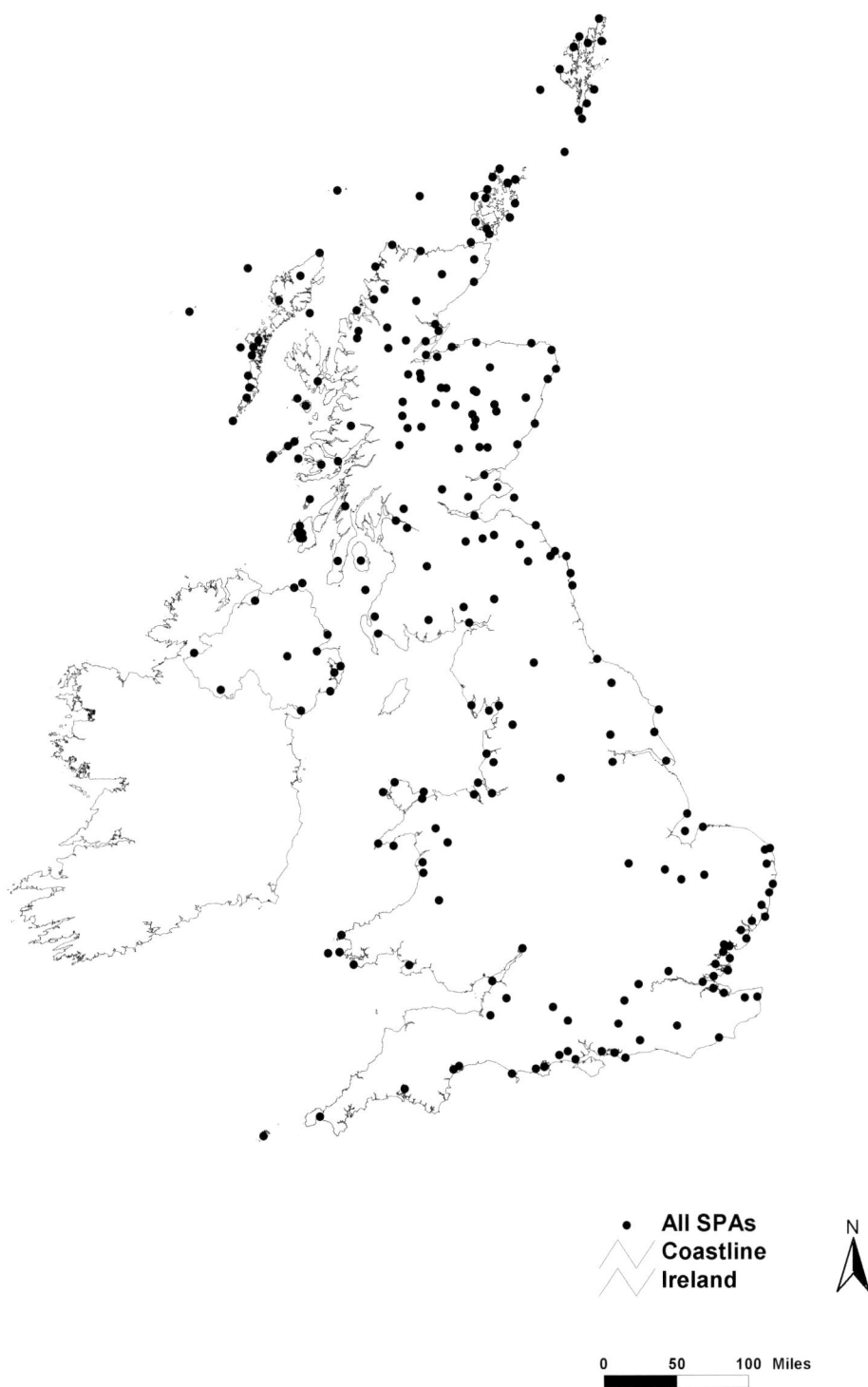

Map showing the UK network of Special Protection Areas. (For more detailed regional maps see Appendix 7.)

1 Introduction

This review represents the UK's contribution to the Natura 2000 network for terrestrial Special Protection Areas. It draws on an extensive background of ornithological surveys undertaken over many years, and previous lists of important sites. It distils best available information concerning species' conservation requirements as stated by Article 4 of the Directive as well as knowledge of internationally important sites for birds in the UK.

The carefully selected network resulting from this review is of large size, contains a wide variety of habitats and includes sites spread throughout the UK. It is logically and scientifically derived, collectively robust, and therefore able to make an enduring contribution to conserving Britain's birds. We recognise, however, the need to be aware of and respond to major biological changes, in particular those consequent upon climate change, or to the availability of significant new data.

1.1 The 'Birds Directive' and Special Protection Areas

In 1979, the European Community adopted the Council Directive on the Conservation of Wild Birds (79/409/EEC). This Directive (see Appendix 2) is usually referred to as the Birds Directive. It provides for the protection, management and control of naturally occurring wild birds within the European Union through a range of mechanisms. One of the key provisions is the establishment of an internationally co-ordinated network of protected areas.

Article 4 of the Birds Directive requires Member States to identify and classify in particular, the most suitable territories in size and number for rare or vulnerable species[1] listed in Annex I (Article 4.1), and for regularly occurring migratory species (Article 4.2). Member States are also required to pay particular attention to the protection of wetlands, especially wetlands of international importance. These sites have become known throughout the Member States as Special Protection Areas (SPAs). Within SPAs, Member States are obliged to take necessary steps to avoid deterioration of natural habitats and disturbance of the species, where this disturbance would be significant having regard to the objectives of the Directive.

The Directive envisages that the classification of SPAs by all Member States will result in a European network of protected sites. This SPA network, together with Special Areas of Conservation under the Habitats Directive, is known as 'Natura 2000'.

1.2 The UK avifauna – features of outstanding international importance

The UK's geographic position – a north temperate island close to a major continental land-mass – results in its particular European importance for a number of groups of birds. Whilst many species or

---

1 The Directive lists some sub-species (*e.g.* Fair Isle Wren and Greenland White-fronted Goose) on Annex I. Throughout this review, reference to the term 'species' should be taken to include such sub-species unless specifically stated to the contrary.

populations occur in internationally important numbers, there are various groups of birds that are of outstanding importance.

- The UK is exceptionally important for many populations of breeding seabirds. Together with Ireland, the UK holds over half the relevant biogeographic (and in some cases, the world) populations of Manx Shearwater[2], Storm Petrel, Gannet, Great Skua, Lesser Black-backed Gull and Puffin (Lloyd *et al.* 1991).

- Britain is the wintering area for many waterbirds (ducks, geese, swans, waders) breeding throughout Arctic and sub-Arctic areas. Birds visiting the UK come from as far afield as the central Canadian Arctic (110 °W) and central Siberia (110 °E). Most of these waterbirds nest at very low densities over extensive areas of the arctic but gather in winter in UK wetlands in dense aggregations. The UK thus has significant international responsibility for high proportions of total populations.

- For many other waterbirds, the UK is not their final destination but is a stepping-stone on their migratory flyways to ultimate winter destinations in Africa. For many waders – such as Ringed Plover, Black-tailed Godwit, Redshank, Sanderling, Dunlin and Knot – the coast of the UK is of crucial importance during the spring and autumn passage periods.

- The British uplands have a unique and characteristic bird community (Ratcliffe 1990, 1991; Brown & Bainbridge 1995). Species such as Golden Plover and Merlin probably nest at higher densities in the British uplands than anywhere else in Europe (Ratcliffe & Thompson 1988), whilst several Arctic breeding birds, such as Red-throated Diver, are at the southern edge of their breeding range.

- The ancient Caledonian pine-forests of the central Scottish Highlands contain Britain's only endemic bird species, the Scottish Crossbill.

---

2 Taxonomy and scientific names used in this report follow the British Ornithologist's Union (BOU 1992, as annually updated) and are given in each species account (Appendix 6).

2 The identification of the UK's SPA network

2.1 Implementation of Article 4 by the UK

The UK has had an active programme of SPA identification and classification since the Birds Directive came into force. The programme has evolved over time, with the progressive development of processes and procedures related to the identification of sites and their classification.

Progress has been hampered, however, by the absence of formally agreed criteria or selection guidelines at EU level. The accession of additional Member States has resulted in revision of the lists of species in the annexes to the Directive (Appendix 2). In the context of the current review, the revisions of 1985 and 1992 were significant, adding to Annex I several species that occurred in the UK.

In implementing Article 4, the UK has had regard to conservation measures taken by other European Union Member States. However, published data on the content of other national SPA networks are not easily available. This has limited the practical extent to which the selection of SPAs by the UK has been influenced by similar activity in other countries.

Throughout the implementation process, the UK government has periodically published lists of qualifying SPAs in *Hansard* and elsewhere[1]. The total number of sites has varied from one listing to another, with an underlying upward trend, reflecting progressively better survey information (see table). Simple comparison of site-lists can be very misleading however, since a number of small sites identified separately in early lists have since been subsumed in larger composite SPAs. These subsumed sites still exist as legal entities although they are not used for reporting purposes, as explained in Appendix 8. The true comparison is the area identified as qualifying for SPA status. This has increased significantly since the early 1980s and the SPA network now amounts to about 1,454,500 ha.

Year	Coverage	No. of Sites
1987	GB	192
1988	GB	188
1991	GB	218
1992	UK	256
2001	UK	243

In 1990, the Nature Conservancy Council (NCC) published its recommendations regarding the proposed network of SPAs in Great Britain (Stroud *et al.* 1990a). This summarised the biological rationale for a national network of SPAs, gave locations of sites identified at that time and provided an assessment of the proportions of populations that would be covered by the then proposed national network. It also highlighted a number of species that were then inadequately covered by the proposed

---

1 Nature Conservancy Council 1983; Commons Hansard 18 March 1985, col. 340; Commons Hansard 18 July 1985, cols. 241–244; Commons Hansard 11 May 1987, cols. 78–85; Commons Hansard 20 December 1988, cols. 187–191; Stroud *et al.* 1990a; Commons Hansard 11 July 1991, cols. 219–224; Pritchard *et al.* 1992; DoE 1994 (Planning Policy Guidance 9: Nature Conservation); Scottish Office Circular 6/1995.

network. For some of these, further survey and census information has since been undertaken in order to identify additional sites.

In 1989, BirdLife International published a European list of Important Bird Areas (IBAs) (a non-statutory listing maintained by BirdLife International – Grimmett & Jones 1989) which built on the earlier inventory of Osieck & Mörzer Bruyns (1981). For the UK, the list of IBAs was then effectively identical with the list of proposed Special Protection Areas identified by the NCC (Stroud *et al.* 1990a), as similar criteria had been used to draw up the two lists.

Details of each SPA proposed by the 1990 NCC review were published jointly by JNCC, the country agencies and RSPB in 1992 as the UK's Important Bird Areas (Pritchard *et al.* 1992). This site inventory was widely distributed to local government and other statutory bodies. It presented more detail on the sites identified in the 1989 European IBA inventory for the UK and the species for which they were important. (It did, however, include some species that were neither migratory nor listed on Annex I and thus were not relevant in the context of Article 4 of the Directive).

The Joint Working Party on Special Protection Areas and Ramsar sites (also acting as the UK's National Ramsar Committee) has routinely reviewed classification of SPAs and provided a valuable national forum that involves government departments, their agencies and non-governmental organisations. It has regularly discussed aspects of the UK's implementation of the Birds Directive.

In 1991, the Office of Public Works, Dublin, and the Department of the Environment for Northern Ireland asked JNCC to advise them with respect to the establishment of an all-Ireland network of SPAs. This review was published in 1993 and gave details of proposed sites and the proportion of all-Ireland populations that would be covered by the suggested network (Way *et al.* 1993).

Since 1992, there has been a range of new ornithological surveys undertaken throughout the UK, especially in the uplands and related to a number of species that were highlighted as being poorly represented in the national network proposed in the early 1990s. In view of new information and possible gaps, Government requested JNCC to review the UK SPA network with a view to recommending a definitive list of sites, identified against explicit selection guidelines.

After a period of consideration and consultation with non-governmental organisations represented on the UK Joint Working Party on SPAs and Ramsar sites, JNCC published the UK's SPA selection guidelines in 1999 (JNCC 1999). The background to the derivation of these guidelines is outlined in section 3.1 and the overall review presented in this document.

In March 2000, BirdLife International published a two-volume updated inventory of IBAs in Europe (Heath & Evans 2000). This again presents a list of IBAs for each European country including the UK. BirdLife International has recently developed uniform global criteria for IBA selection which differ from those previously used in the UK (Pritchard *et al.* 1992). Accordingly, the list of IBAs published by BirdLife in the current review (Heath & Evans 2000) is no longer identical to the UK SPA network presented here. Notwithstanding the minor differences, there is, however, a broad degree of similarity between the SPA and IBA lists for the UK. Indeed, data from the draft IBA inventory for the UK were used in preparatory work for this SPA review.

The minor differences between the IBA and SPA lists for the UK are unsurprising and to be expected since different selection guidelines, criteria, time-periods and priorities have been used to identify the respective site networks. In cases where there are significant differences between boundaries of IBAs and SPAs, the reasons for these differences are always clearly justified in the context of the requirements of the Birds Directive.

2.2 Geographical scope of this review

This review presents the national network of SPAs in the terrestrial environment of England, Scotland, Wales and Northern Ireland. There has been a long tradition of cross-border co-operation between the Republic of Ireland and Northern Ireland regarding nature conservation matters. As often as possible, the biogeographic entity of the whole of Ireland is used as the context for conservation priority setting (*e.g.* Whilde *et al.* 1993). Indeed, the previous review of SPAs in Ireland was jointly commissioned by government departments in both the Republic and Northern Ireland (Way *et al.* 1993).

The Directive's obligations cover all the territory of Member States and therefore include the marine environment. This review has considered terrestrial sites that extend partly into marine or intertidal areas, for example, in estuaries. It has not, however, considered the requirements of birds using the wholly offshore environment, and proposed marine SPAs are not presented here. The protection requirements of birds in the offshore marine environment (with respect to Article 4) are outside the scope of this review.

2.3 Data-handling issues

The site and species data used in this review have come from a wide variety of sources. The overall aim was to obtain the best-available 'snapshot' of information about sites and species in the mid-1990s to enable the resulting site series to sit in a uniform context. Because of the periodic nature of national surveys, data for different groups of species have not always been derived from exactly the same years. Generally, however, data mostly relate to the five-year period 1991/92 to 1995/96, unless there have been compelling reasons to use earlier or later data. These were the most current data available at the commencement of the review.

At an early stage, definitive reference population sizes were agreed for relevant breeding, passage and wintering populations, and geographical scales (Great Britain, all-Ireland and international). The reference populations for each species – which were taken from published sources available at the commencement of the review – are set out in Appendix 4.

A large number of issues surrounding data sources, and qualifying species, arose during the production of this review. These are explained in more detail in Appendix 5.

2.4 Future monitoring

Article 4 of the Birds Directive states that *"trends and variations in populations shall be taken into account as a background"* by Member States in the evaluation of their special conservation measures. This indicates the need for monitoring of species status at a variety of scales.

The UK has in place arguably the most comprehensive regime of bird monitoring in the world. Detailed monitoring is undertaken on many sites through schemes such as the Wetland Bird Survey and the Seabird Colony Register. This monitoring provides essential feedback on the performance and efficacy of the SPA network as a whole, as well as aiding managers of individual sites to assess the success of site management regimes. It will also enable the UK to be aware of major biological changes, in particular those consequent upon current changes of climate.

3 Selection guidelines for Special Protection Areas

3.1 Background to derivation

The process of selecting SPAs in the UK has been hindered by the lack of agreed selection criteria formalised at a European scale. Selection guidelines for the UK have, therefore, been derived from knowledge of common international practice. The selection guidelines below – which are based on scientific criteria – were prepared to assist the selection of SPAs in the UK. They were published by JNCC in 1999 on behalf of the statutory agencies and government departments concerned.

In order to maintain conformity and common standards, the UK has had regard to the internationally agreed guidelines for the selection of wetlands of international importance under the Ramsar Convention. The SPA guidelines make explicit reference to a number of definitions and other principles relating to Ramsar site selection guidance[1].

The selection guidelines were applied to available data in two stages (described in more detail in section 4):

(1)   the first stage identified areas likely to qualify for SPA status;

(2)   the second stage considered these areas further using one or more of the judgements in Stage 2 to select the most suitable areas in number and size for SPA classification.

Stage 1's fourth guideline allows consideration, using the Stage 2 judgements, to be given to cases where a species' population status, ecology or movement patterns may mean that an adequate number of areas cannot be identified from Stage 1's first three guidelines alone. The Stage 2 judgements were particularly important for selecting and determining the boundaries of SPAs for thinly dispersed and wide-ranging species.

In the application of Stage 2 judgements, preference was given to those areas that contributed significantly to the species' population viability both locally and as a whole. The protection of the populations in SPAs was considered alongside, and is complemented by other non-site-based special measures designed to maintain populations (section 6).

---

1   The most recent guidance for the selection of Ramsar sites, and revised criteria, was agreed at the seventh
    Conference of Parties in 1999 – Resolution C.7.11 (Ramsar Convention Bureau 2000).

3.2 The Guidelines

Stage 1

(1)   An area is used regularly by 1% or more of the Great Britain (or in Northern Ireland, the all-Ireland) population of a species listed in Annex I of the Birds Directive (79/409/EEC as amended) in any season.

(2)   An area is used regularly by 1% or more of the biogeographical population of a regularly occurring migratory species (other than those listed in Annex I) in any season.

(3)   An area is used regularly by over 20,000 waterfowl (waterfowl as defined by the Ramsar Convention) or 20,000 seabirds in any season.

(4)   An area which meets the requirements of one or more of the Stage 2 guidelines in any season, where the application of Stage 1 guidelines 1, 2 or 3 for a species does not identify an adequate suite of most suitable sites for the conservation of that species.

Stage 2

(1)   *Population size and density*
      Areas holding or supporting more birds than others and/or holding or supporting birds at higher concentrations are favoured for selection.

(2)   *Species range*
      Areas selected for a given species provide as wide a geographic coverage across the species' range as possible.

(3)   *Breeding success*
      Areas of higher breeding success than others are favoured for selection.

(4)   *History of occupancy*
      Areas known to have a longer history of occupation or use by the relevant species are favoured for selection.

(5)   *Multi-species areas*
      Areas holding or supporting the larger number of qualifying species under Article 4 of the Directive are favoured for selection.

(6)   *Naturalness*
      Areas comprising natural or semi-natural habitats are favoured for selection over those which do not.

(7)   *Severe weather refuges*
      Areas used at least once a decade by significant proportions of the biogeographical population of a species in periods of severe weather in any season, and which are vital to the survival of a viable population, are favoured for selection.

4 Applying the SPA selection guidelines

The application of the selection guidelines has generated the list of SPAs set out in Appendix 7. The section below explains the methods and approach adopted in selecting the list of UK SPAs and their qualifying features. The species accounts in Appendix 6 summarise the reasons why the particular suite of SPAs has been selected for each species. They also include information about each species' population status, size and distribution, and population structure and trends.

Following the agreement of site selection guidelines, JNCC convened a series of inter-agency review workshops in January 1998, which assessed the suite of sites for each regularly occurring Annex I species, and each regularly occurring migratory species (see Appendix 5.1).

The requirements of each species were assessed against a 'decision-tree' (see Figure 4.1). For many species, the initial meetings highlighted the need for further work to identify additional possible sites, and/or add further qualifying species to existing sites. The process of reviewing species site requirements was substantially completed by June 1999.

4.1 Selection Stage 1.1

4.1.1 'National' population estimates and thresholds

For Annex I species, 1% thresholds relate to national rather than international population numbers. 'National' populations have been defined separately for Great Britain and for all-Ireland as two separate biogeographic entities, reflecting a long-established approach (Way *et al.* 1993).

For Great Britain, thresholds were derived from breeding or non-breeding population estimates collated by Stone *et al.* (1997), except for Hen Harrier, Stone Curlew, Greenshank and Woodlark. The assessment of 483 pairs derived from the 1988 national survey of Hen Harriers (Sim *et al.* 1999, in press) was used as the most recent national context. For Stone Curlew, an unpublished national total for 1998 was used (English Nature unpublished), whilst for Greenshank, the total of 1,440 pairs derived from the 1997 national stratified sample survey (Hancock *et al.* 1997) was adopted. For Woodlark, the more recent population estimate of 1,500 pairs derived from the British Trust for Ornithology (BTO) national survey of 1997 (Wotton & Gillings 2000) was used.

For all-Ireland populations, thresholds for non-breeding waterfowl used by Way *et al.* (1993) were used, whilst for other species thresholds were calculated from all-Ireland population estimates made by Gibbons *et al.* (1993).

4.1.2 Minimum numbers for wintering waterbirds

The size of the national population of some wintering waterbirds is very small. This typically is the case for those species whose main range in the non-breeding season occurs either to the south (*e.g.* for Ruff and Greenshank) or east (*e.g.* Bean Goose and Smew) of the UK. For these species, 1% of national populations give small values, often amounting to just a few individuals. In an international context

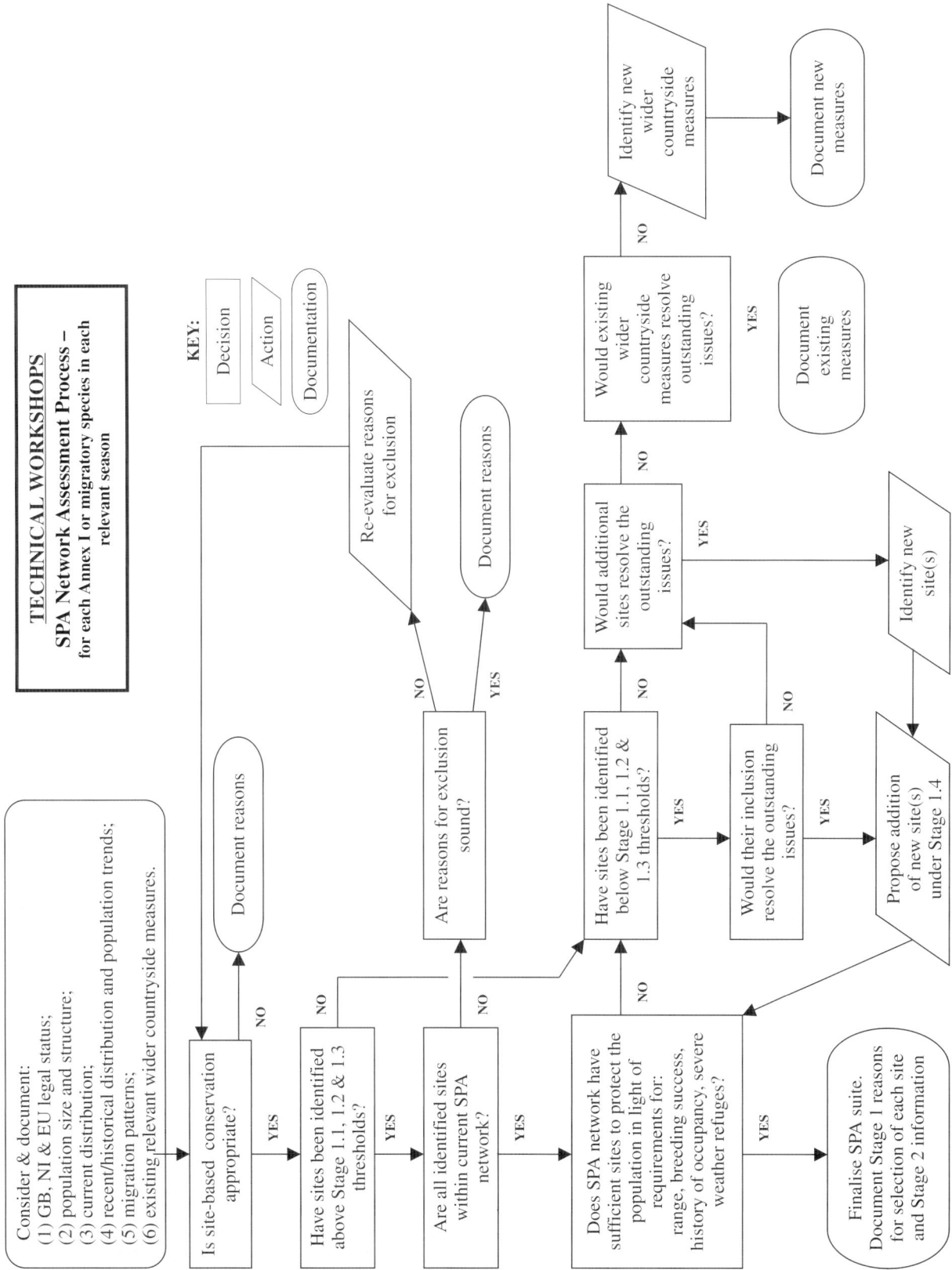

Figure 4.1

these very small numbers are not of major significance for sustaining viable biogeographical populations of these species.

With this in mind, it has been the statutory agencies' long-standing practice to require at least 50 individuals to be regularly present on a site before that area is considered for site selection (Salmon 1981). This has been the practice with regard to the selection of SSSIs and has also been adopted for this review of SPAs.

Note that the guideline has only been applied in the context of wintering waterbirds. It would not be appropriate for breeding birds where the rarest breeding populations of many species are characterised by just a few pairs. Nor would it be appropriate where the global population size is small (for example, a globally threatened species of waterbird such as Bittern). In such a case, it would be entirely appropriate to select a site based on small absolute numbers (asindeed, is urged by the Ramsar Convention's site selection guidance – Res. C.VII.11).

4.2 Selection Stage 1.2

Whilst Guideline 1.1 selects the most important sites in the UK for Annex I species, Guideline 1.2 selects the most important sites at flyway scale. In this way, the number of UK sites selected under this guideline reflect the proportional responsibility the UK has for the species concerned. Significant numbers of sites have been selected for those species where the UK holds the major part of their international population (*e.g.* Pintail and many of the goose populations).

4.2.1 International population estimates and thresholds

For UK waterbirds, the recommended 1% thresholds published by Rose & Scott (1997) have been used, except for the following species.

For Red-breasted Merganser, Scott & Rose (1996) recommended the treatment of birds occurring in East Greenland, Iceland, Britain and Ireland as a separate biogeographical population. However, for reasons given in species account A6.42, the review has followed the earlier treatment of Rose & Scott (1994), which groups British Red-breasted Mergansers with others from north-west and central Europe, giving a 1% threshold of 1,250.

The British breeding population of Goosander is non-migratory, although these birds are joined in winter by others regularly migrating from Scandinavia (Boyd 1959; Owen *et al.* 1986). Accordingly, SPAs have been selected to cover aggregations in the non-breeding season, but not the breeding period.

For taxa other than waterbirds, there are fewer compiled data and no regular international summary of population sizes. For birds of prey, international totals for each species in European countries west of the Urals[1] were calculated from data in Hagemeijer & Blair (1997) and reported by the DETR/JNCC Raptor Working Group (2000 – Table 2.3).

4.3 Selection Stage 1.3

4.3.1 Definition of important assemblage components

Guidelines 1.1 and 1.2 refer to numbers of a particular species at a site, whilst guideline 1.3 covers total numbers of *all* species within a defined assemblage at a site. All migratory and Annex I waterbirds within an assemblage are qualifying species. The main component species that characterise particular assemblages have been identified. To achieve this, 1% of national populations was used to provide basic guidance. In other words, at sites holding at least 20,000 waterbirds, species have been listed in this review where at least 1% of a national population is present within the assemblage.

---

1 The definition of Europe used in this context includes the islands of the Azores, Madeira and the Canaries, Russia east to the Urals, and the Caucasus, but excludes the whole of Turkey.

This approach, however, does not highlight the presence within internationally important assemblages of those species with very large national populations (and hence very large 1% national thresholds). This relates especially to Lapwing and more occasionally Wigeon, Dunlin, Knot and Oystercatcher. These species may rank as the primary or secondary component of a site's waterbird assemblage but despite many thousands being present, numbers are less than 1% of national populations. In order for species to qualify as a listed component of an assemblage, their numbers had to exceed 10% of the minimum qualifying assemblage of 20,000 individuals (*i.e.* at least 2,000 individuals). The same rules were adopted for assemblages of seabirds.

4.3.2 Single species assemblages

For the purposes of SPA classification and this review, the presence of 20,000 or more individuals of a single species on a site was not considered to fulfil the definition of an 'assemblage'. For SPA classification purposes, assemblages have had to include more than one species within the relevant season. Thus, a site holding 28,000 individual breeding Black-headed Gulls alone (comprising only 0.8% of international population) would not be considered to fulfil guideline 1.3.

4.3.3 Breeding seabirds

In the breeding season, 20,000 seabirds are taken as equating to 10,000 pairs (or other standard units such as apparently occupied nest sites/territories as appropriate for some species – Lloyd *et al.* 1991).

4.4 Selection Stage 1.4

The Directive requires Member States to select the *"most suitable territories"* as sites for SPA classification. Initial selections were made using guidelines 1.1–1.3. Guideline 1.4 gives latitude for the exercise of scientific judgement where the application of guidelines 1.1–1.3 are considered to identify insufficient SPAs, and if site-based protection is an appropriate conservation response for the species, sites may be selected. Generally, this is through the addition of the species as a qualifying feature, following consideration of Stage 2 judgements, to SPAs classified for other species. If no such site within the existing network can be identified, and a robust case can be made, then a new, single-species site may be identified (as has occurred, for example, for Leach's Petrel and Cormorant).

Guideline 1.4 has been used to select SPA suites (in whole or in part) for the following species: Leach's Petrel, breeding Cormorant, Bean Goose, Pink-footed Goose, breeding Wigeon, Scaup, breeding Common Scoter, breeding and wintering Hen Harrier, breeding Merlin, breeding Peregrine, Corncrake, breeding and wintering Oystercatcher, breeding Golden Plover, breeding Ringed Plover, Sanderling, Purple Sandpiper, breeding Dunlin, breeding Black-tailed Godwit, breeding Whimbrel, breeding Redshank, breeding Greenshank, Little Tern and Arctic Skua.

4.5 Site boundaries

The UK SPA network consists of 243 sites covering a wide variety of different habitats, ranging from offshore seabird stacks and cliffs, to estuaries and lowland heathland. It is beyond the scope of this report to deal comprehensively with the issue of determining boundaries for these SPAs because unique issues usually arise at each site. This section outlines the general principles underlying boundary determination.

In many cases, SPAs have been selected which are distinct in habitat and/or ornithological importance from the surroundings and have definable and recognisable character (*i.e.* the specific boundary is clearly identifiable 'on the ground'). They must also provide for the conservation requirements of the species in the season(s) and for the particular purposes for which they are classified. This process involves informed scientific judgement to define the most suitable territories (*i.e.* SPAs).

4.5.1 Site boundaries and the SPA review

The application of the first stage of the SPA guidelines identifies broad areas of interest or potential ornithological importance. The application of the Stage 2 judgements, however, requires more precise locational information since this process involves between-site comparisons of numbers, densities and other attributes that depend on exact area assessments. Thus, Stage 2 is integrally linked with the determination of site boundaries for the qualifying species as outlined below.

4.5.2 General principles

The first stage of boundary determination involves defining the extent of area required by the qualifying species concerned. These scientific judgements are made in the light of the ecological requirements of the relevant species that may be delivered by that particular site, and the extent to which the site can fulfil these requirements. This follows a rigorous assessment of best-available local information regarding distribution, abundance and movements of the qualifying species. It may also involve the commissioning of special surveys where the information base is weak.

Following this stage, every attempt is made to define a boundary that is identifiable on the ground and can be recognised by those responsible for the management of the site. This boundary will include the most suitable areas for the qualifying species identified in the first stage, but will relate to landscape features such as changes in habitat, field boundaries, rivers, roads *etc.*, and thus may be marginally more extensive.

Some SPAs consist of a cluster of smaller units sometimes separated from each other by significant distance. Where this occurs it is often for one or more of the following reasons:

(1)   where site elements are ecologically linked in their use by a common bird population (*e.g.* a group of alternative roost or feeding areas used by one population of waterbirds); and/or

(2)   where habitat was formerly geographically continuous before being separated by human activity (as for example heathland areas now fragmented).

(3)   where breeding birds are widely separated by the presence of habitats not directly contributing to their conservation, accordingly, these areas have been excluded in site definitions.

In cases where species' requirements are not met entirely by means of SPA classification, additional provision is achieved through other policies (for example agri-environment incentives to manage areas surrounding SPAs in an environmentally sensitive manner).

4.5.3 Modifications to site boundaries

Over the period since the implementation of the Birds Directive, detailed knowledge both of UK bird species and of sites has grown. In the light of these improvements in understanding, it has sometimes been found necessary to extend the scope of some initial classifications (Appendix 8).

4.6 Stage 2 judgements

The Stage 1 guidelines have been used to identify possible sites for SPA classification, whereas the Stage 2 judgements have been used to decide which are the most 'suitable' (in the sense of Article 4.1 of the Birds Directive). Those sites meeting several of the Stage 2 judgements have not necessarily been selected in preference to those meeting only one. This is because the factors operate independently as indicators of the various different kinds of importance that a site may have.

4.6.1 Population size and density

Comparisons of population sizes have been undertaken on a simple numerical basis, for non-breeding waterbirds using five-year peak mean counts (where these were available). Different means of calculating densities were applied to different species as appropriate.

4.6.2 Species range

In order to maintain range, SPAs have been selected to represent the extremities and the main centre(s) of the range, and principle occurrences in relevant regions of the UK.

Some species such as Pink-footed Goose and Icelandic Greylag Goose (species accounts A6.18 and A6.21) move across the country in the course of the non-breeding season and thus have a dynamic distribution. In such cases, the selection of sites has been undertaken on a regional basis to ensure that the main centres of occurrence are all represented within respective SPA suites.

4.6.3 Breeding success

The role of one site in providing birds for other areas – *i.e.* its success as a source – is generally judged by absolute measures of productivity at the breeding site rather than evidence of its known contribution of birds, by dispersal, to other locations. Thus, recruitment to other areas is generally inferred from high productivity at the source rather than known occupation at the destination (information which is usually unavailable). Extremely limited data exist to apply this judgement, although it has been applied where appropriate to select sites for species such as Black-throated Diver, Slavonian Grebe and Golden Eagle where information on productivity at different sites exists.

4.6.4 History of occupancy

Sites with a long history of occupancy are normally favourable to species. There are, however, some important exceptions to this. For example, some birds use successional habitats and favourable conditions may occur only for a limited number of years. In such situations, recently occupied sites can be especially important in ensuring the survival and reproduction of some birds. This Stage 2 judgement has, therefore, been applied with caution in the light of such ecological requirements.

At an early stage in the review, the Project Steering Group agreed to adopt the period of the first BTO Breeding Bird Atlas – 1968–1972 (Sharrock 1976) – as the baseline against which to assess history of occupancy. Any site occupied for the first time more recently than 1972 has not, therefore, been considered as having a long history of occupation in the context of this guideline.

Certain colonial nesting species, particularly terns, regularly move between different nesting sites from year to year. Thus, numbers at any one site can fluctuate from several hundred pairs to zero and back within the space of a few years (Sears & Avery 1993). Terns have, therefore, been retained as qualifying species on a number of sites where contemporary numbers are very low (below current qualification thresholds) but where there is a history of occupancy and/or where a site is known to be part of a large complex of nesting areas.

4.6.5 Multi-species areas

The favouring of sites with larger numbers of qualifying species has regard for complementarity theory (Pressey *et al.* 1993; Pressey 1996; see Appendix 1), although this has not been formally applied in this review. Multi-species sites are important since the large number of species supported on such sites is typically an attribute of areas of high conservation importance. Generally, multi-species sites are large and often contain a diverse mosaic of high-quality habitats. Such areas provide a degree of ecological complexity that support many species at levels of international importance.

The distinctive ecology of some species means that they rarely occur together with other species at levels of European importance. For example, most SPAs selected for Black-throated Diver contain only that species at qualifying levels. This judgement has been applied carefully in order to avoid inappropriately 'downgrading' the status of some single-species sites, which may be of critical importance for a species in a way that a multiple-species site may not.

4.6.6 Naturalness

As a general rule, sites having a low degree of naturalness (for example, urban and other industrialised landscapes) have not been selected for SPA classification. However, some 'less natural' sites, with large numbers of species or high species diversity, have been chosen as SPAs. This, typically, reflects appropriate management over long periods that has benefited the species concerned. Such areas include low-intensity and small-scale arable areas (which can be of particular importance for species such as Corncrake and Stone Curlew) and some water storage reservoirs.

4.6.7 Severe weather refuges

Severe weather in winter can result in the displacement of birds from their normal haunts to areas (usually in the south or west) which are subject to milder conditions. Some species readily move long distances to find more favourable areas at the onset of hard conditions, whilst others, for example Oystercatcher, tend to stay and 'gamble' that local food supplies will last for the duration of the cold (Meininger *et al.* 1991; Camphuysen *et al.* 1996).

Following several periods of severe cold weather in the 1980s, Ridgill & Fox (1990) reviewed cold weather movements of Mallard, Teal, Wigeon, Pintail, Shoveler, Pochard, Tufted Duck, Shelduck and Coot in western Europe. This highlighted the major importance of British west coast estuaries for those wildfowl and waders displaced in cold periods from eastern Britain and continental Europe. SPAs have been selected to reflect this. The 1990s were generally a period of milder winters and the analyses undertaken by Ridgill & Fox (1990) have yet to be made for other wildfowl or for wader species.

4.7 Species for which SPA suites will require future review

There are a very small number of species that, for reasons outlined below, it has not yet been possible to identify full SPA suites. These will require further review. There are three main reasons for this:

● it is too early to assess 'most suitable' sites for species that are actively expanding in range and population size in the UK;

● lack of suitable data and information with which to assess important sites;

● the protection requirements of birds in the offshore marine environment are outside the scope of this review.

4.7.1 Recent UK colonists

A number of species have colonised the UK in recent years, predominantly from mainland Europe. For example, Little Egret was a regular but rare vagrant in the UK until large influxes began in 1989. Since then, numbers have continued to increase and the species is found at wide-ranging sites along the coast of southern and south-eastern England (see species account A6.14). In 1996, it bred in the UK for the first time. The SPA suite for this species reflects the current size and distribution of the population in each season. Given the continuing expansion of the population size and range, however, a review of its SPA suite is likely to be required at a future date. The Rare Breeding Birds Panel and the Wetland Bird Survey will provide the necessary data for such a review.

4.7.2 Re-establishing raptors

Both White-tailed Eagle and Red Kite are currently undergoing significant expansions in their UK populations and distribution arising from re-establishment schemes which commenced in the late 1980s (Evans *et al.* 1994). Within the UK, the Red Kite's current SPA provision maintains the native core population in Wales. A suite of SPAs for Red Kites may be appropriate in England and Scotland in the future, when populations in these countries have increased to such an extent that the 'most suitable' sites can be determined. Data from the Rare Birds Breeding Panel and the proposed decennial national survey of Red Kites (commencing in 2000) will provide the necessary data for such a review.

4.7.3 Wintering gulls

The review discovered that for gull species, data were not available to undertake a comprehensive assessment of their distribution and need for SPA protection during the winter period. Data from the most recent (decennial) national gull roost survey undertaken by the BTO in 1993 are unpublished. The Wetland Bird Survey (WeBS) began collecting data on wintering gulls in 1993 (Cranswick *et al.*

1995) and when suitable data are available allowing regularity at key sites to be assessed, it is intended to review SPA suites for these species. In the light of this data inadequacy, JNCC will be working to further develop WeBS monitoring to better assess wintering gull numbers, and identify important sites in a national context.

4.7.4 Wintering raptors in coastal areas

Information on the distribution and numbers of Hen Harriers and Merlins in winter, especially in coastal areas, is currently limited. Where information is available, this has been used to identify suites of SPAs for these species. JNCC and the country agencies will work to develop better monitoring of wintering raptors in the UK, at both site and national scales. It is possible that further sites of European importance for Hen Harrier and Merlin will be identified through this work.

4.7.5 Passage waders and terns

The estuaries and rocky-shore coasts of the UK are important to waders not just during the winter period, but also during the autumn and spring migration periods. For some species, for example Sanderling and Ringed Plover, peak numbers recorded nationally occur in April-May or in August-October. Whilst WeBS collects data at some sites during these passage periods, they are not normally published annually and have only been systematically collected at most coastal sites since 1993 (Cranswick *et al.* 1995). The issues involved with interpretation of data during periods of high turnover (Frederiksen *et al.* 2001) and in situations where mixed populations (such as three populations of Dunlins) may be present, are also far from clear. Indeed, such situations may present intractable fieldwork problems. Where data relating to passage periods have been readily available, however, they have been used in this review.

The comprehensive database being developed by WeBS will allow much better interpretation of existing UK passage data for waterbirds (including Ringed Plover, Redshank, Curlew and Sanderling). It seems unlikely that new sites will be identified, but some species may be added as qualifying species to existing SPAs, where there is a large passage occurrence but limited overwintering.

Similar issues apply to terns on migration. Those breeding in northern parts of the UK use more southerly estuaries en route to wintering areas off the coasts of Africa. Knowledge of these autumn (and spring) movements is poor and the list of sites identified in this review is known to be incomplete. JNCC will review existing knowledge on important sites in the UK for waders and terns. The WeBS partnership is also actively taking steps to ensure that those sites of importance in any season of the year, and which are subject to monitoring, are clearly identified in annual published reports.

4.7.6 Marine species

Whilst this review has considered terrestrial sites that extend into marine or intertidal areas for example, estuaries or inshore areas – it has not considered the requirements of birds using the wholly offshore environment. The site suites presented here may be incomplete and possible additional provision still needs to be determined in the marine environment. The protection requirements of birds in the offshore marine environment (with respect to Article 4 of the Birds Directive) will be considered in a separate review being co-ordinated by JNCC.

4.8 Species for which SPAs are inappropriate

There are a number of species where site-based measures are not an appropriate protection mechanism, or it is simply not feasible to identify the 'most suitable sites'. Where this is the case, it has been stated in the relevant species accounts. Typically, these species fall into the following categories:

4.8.1 Species that are broadly dispersed

Many migratory birds are broadly dispersed and do not occur in significant aggregations. Site-based measures under the Birds Directive are not, therefore, appropriate for their population conservation.

These include typical summer migrants, such as Swallow, House Martin, Chiffchaff and Willow Warbler, as well as winter migrants such as Redwing, Fieldfare, Lapland Bunting and Snow Bunting.

4.8.2 Species that are sedentary year-round

The Bonn Convention on the Conservation of Migratory Species of Wild Animals defines migratory species as *"the entire population or any geographically separate part of the population of any species or lower taxon of wild animals, a significant proportion of whose members cyclically and predictably cross one or more national jurisdictional boundaries"*. The BTO were asked to advise on the application of this definition to the UK avifauna and their findings are summarised in Appendix 3 (see also Appendix 5.1).

This review has highlighted the fact that certain resident or sedentary species in a UK context were listed as qualifying species on citations of SPAs designated some years ago. In view of the BTO work, the following sedentary species have now been removed as qualifying features from the citations for classified or proposed SPAs: Mute Swan, Black Guillemot, the native north Scottish population of Greylag Geese, Water Rail and Bearded Tit.

4.8.3 Non-native species

There are no requirements under the Birds Directive to take site-based protective measures for non-native bird species.

5 The content of the SPA network

Suites of SPAs have been selected for Annex I and migratory species where this is an appropriate response to conservation needs. The degree to which these suites contain proportions of national populations within the network is assessed below.

Conservation science theory (*e.g.* Shafer 1990; Ramsar Resolution VII.11) and practice suggests that those species where highest proportions of species' populations should be located within a protected area network are those which:

- occur locally in high densities (congregatory species);

- occur, to a large extent, on natural or semi-natural habitats;

- show predictable occurrence at particular sites regularly between years (*i.e.* species that are not irregular or dispersive);

- have restricted national or international ranges; or

- have small national or international population sizes.

A series of analyses have been undertaken to test these presumptions against the results of this review of the UK SPA network.

5.1 Proportions of breeding populations within the UK's SPA network

Proportions of Great Britain populations in the SPA network have been related to the dispersion of these species indicated by the most recent BTO breeding bird atlas (Gibbons *et al.* 1993). Two analyses have been undertaken (Figures 5.1 and 5.2) because different selection thresholds have been adopted for Annex I species compared to other migratory species. The measure of range used was the number of 10 km grid squares in Britain with breeding evidence found in the period 1988–1991. It was not possible to undertake this analysis separately for Northern Ireland since the selection area (all-Ireland) is larger than the area within which SPAs have been selected in this exercise.

The results of this analysis show that there is a strong statistical relationship between both Annex I and breeding migratory species' ranges and the proportion of their British populations within SPA suites. Geographically more restricted birds (those occupying fewest 10 km squares) have increasingly higher proportions of their British breeding populations within SPAs. Indeed, for a number of rare species (*e.g.* Leach's Petrel, Wood Sandpiper, Fair Isle Wren) the whole UK population is contained within SPAs. Many of the colonially breeding seabirds have high percentages of their populations within SPAs, such as Manx Shearwater, Puffin and Lesser Black-backed Gull (all with about 100% population inclusion), Guillemot (92%), Roseate Tern (88%), Kittiwake (78%), Razorbill (76%), Great Skua (74%) and Sandwich Tern (72%). For most of these species breeding occurs at just a few locations (*e.g.* within just 18 10 km squares for Gannet and 22 for Manx Shearwater).

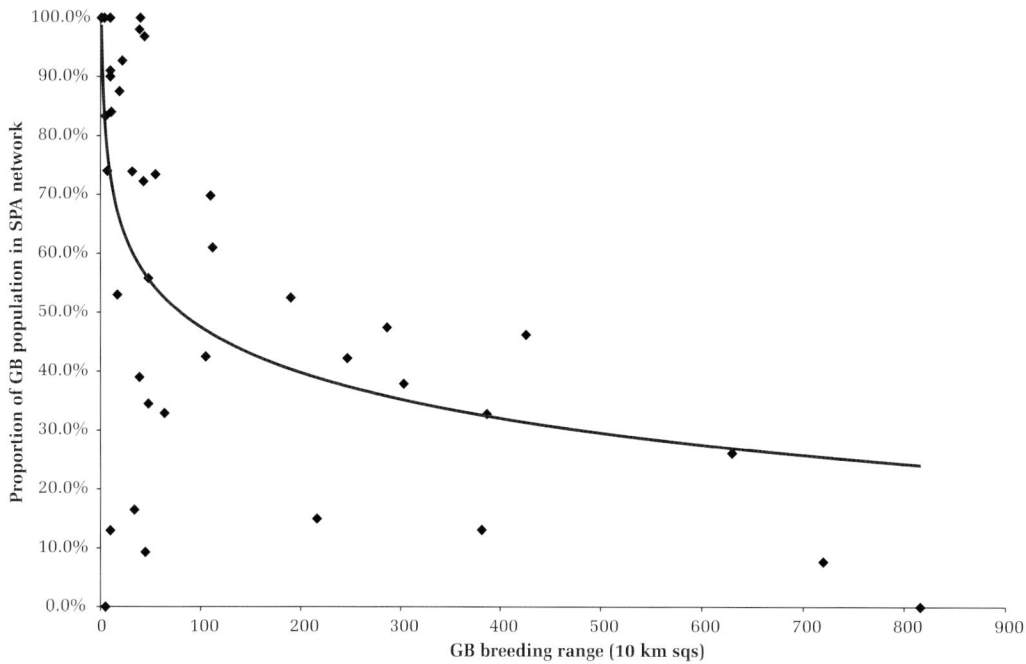

Figure 5.1 Relationship between geographic range within Britain (occupancy of 10 km squares in 1988–1991 – from Gibbons *et al.* 1993) and proportion of British breeding populations contained within SPA suite within Britain for Annex I breeding species. [Logarithmic relationship: $y = -0.1115\text{Ln}(x) + 0.9884$; $R^2 = 0.3126$]

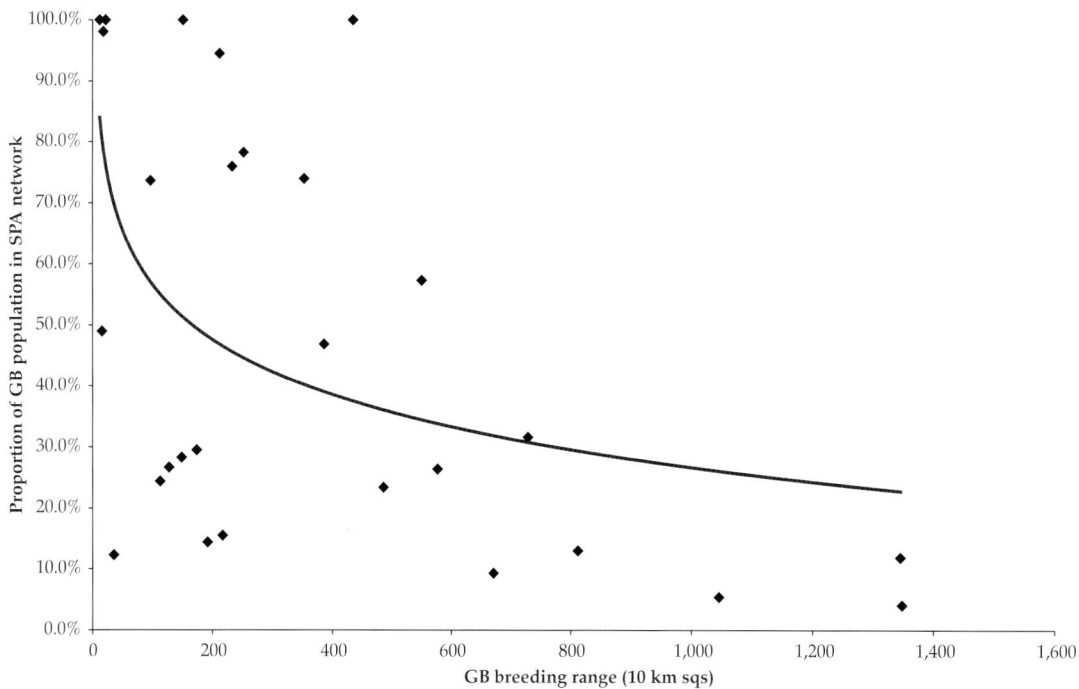

Figure 5.2 Relationship between geographic range within Britain (occupancy of 10 km squares in 1988–1991 – from Gibbons *et al.* 1993) and proportion of British breeding populations contained within SPA suite within Britain for migratory, non-Annex I breeding species. (Migratory species with very large populations and for which no SPAs have been selected (section 6.106) are not plotted.) [Logarithmic relationship: $y = -0.1302\text{Ln}(x) + 1.1658$; $R^2 = 0.2503$]

Conversely, populations that are widely dispersed in the breeding season (*e.g.* Golden Plover, Ringed Plover, Redshank, Merlin and Peregrine) have lower proportional coverage within SPAs.

There are some rare species with low population coverage within SPAs which do not exhibit the parameters indicated above. For these species, site-based protection is not the most appropriate means of conserving viable populations. For example, Montagu's Harrier does not occur within the SPA network even though it has a very low population size. This is because the species occurs at low density, usually on managed farmland, and often in different locations in different years. The identification and classification of SPAs is not, therefore, the most appropriate means of conserving the population, and other measures have been put in place.

Another species that has low proportional occurrence is Red Kite. In the breeding season, this is a non-congregatory species that occurs at low densities. Thus, the identification and classification of sites for a significant proportion of the population is especially problematic. Again, other measures have been put in place to ensure the conservation of the population (see species account A.6.45).

5.2 Proportions of wintering totals within the UK's SPA network

A similar analysis has been undertaken to assess the proportions of total numbers of wintering waterbirds in the SPA network. An index of dispersal in winter was taken as the total number of occupied 10 km grid-squares (or 'hectads') from the 1981/82–1983/84 BTO winter atlas (Lack 1986)[1].

The broad pattern of occurrence within SPAs was similar for both Annex I species (Figure 5.3) and non-Annex I migratory species (Figure 5.4). Those birds with the most restricted distributions (*e.g.* Avocet, Bar-tailed Godwit, Grey Plover, Pintail and Shelduck) have higher proportions of British populations contained within the SPA network. In contrast, widely dispersed species, such as Mallard, Tufted Duck, Coot and Lapwing, are contained within SPAs to a lesser extent.

5.3 Proportions of international populations within the UK's SPA network

One basic tenet of international conservation is that countries have particular responsibility for those species or habitats that occur uniquely or in high proportions within their borders (*e.g.* Dunn *et al.* 1999). Thus, Article 3(2) of the Habitats Directive requires that, for any habitat or species, the national selection of Special Areas of Conservation (SACs) should be proportional to the degree to which that species or habitat is represented within the country concerned. Although the Birds Directive does not have a similar requirement, the degree to which this relationship exists within this review has been assessed (Figure 5.5).

The proportion of the international population of any species/sub-species that occurs within the UK (using data from Annex 4) has been related to the proportion of the UK population occurring within the SPA network (Annex 2). For both Annex I and for non-Annex I migratory species, there is a strong relationship. Those species (or sub-species) for which a large proportion of the international population occurs in the UK also have a high proportion of that population within the SPA network. Examples include Svalbard Barnacle Goose (100% within the UK, 100% within SPAs), Canadian Light-bellied Brent Goose (73% UK, 70% SPAs), Greenland Barnacle Goose (79% UK, 50% SPAs), Pintail (46% UK, 32% SPAs) and Dark-bellied Brent Goose (34% UK, 31% SPAs). Those species whose main population centres in winter lie away from the UK are represented within the network to a lesser extent.

There are two notable exceptions to this relationship. In winter, the UK holds 96% of the international population of Turnstone and 60% of the population of Ringed Plovers, but only 14% and 14% of these

---

1 Although the data from the winter atlas predates the data from the review by about a decade, there have been few significant changes in gross range by wintering waterbirds in the UK in this period. There have been some changes in population sizes, but overall distribution in the mid-1990s was similar to that in the mid-1980s.

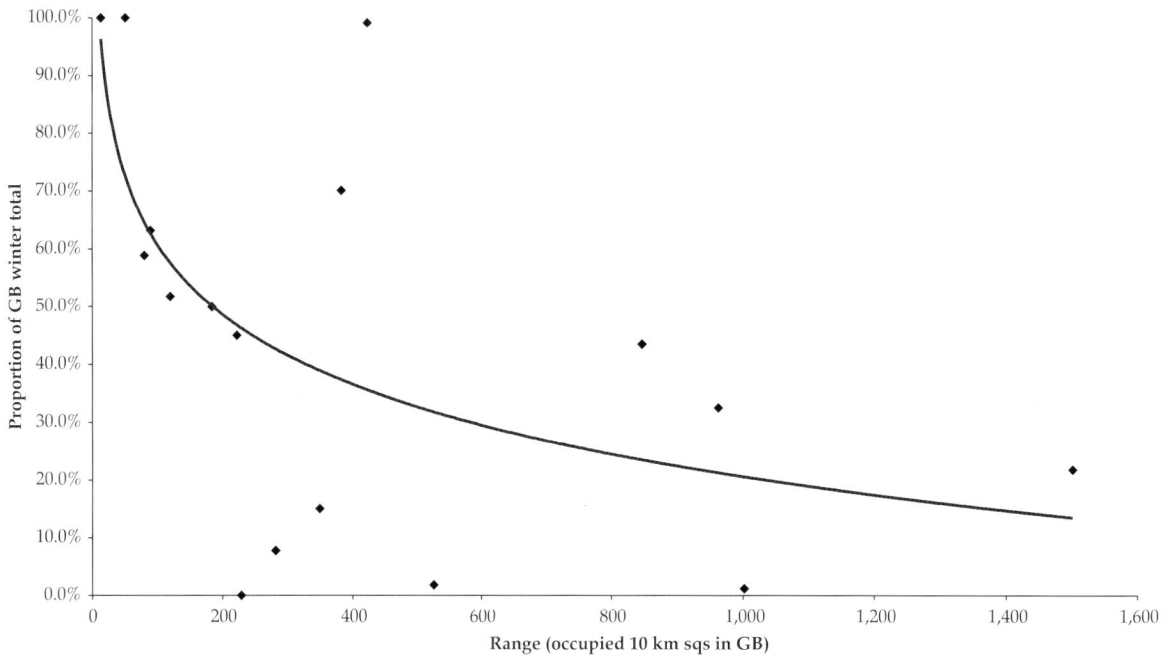

Figure 5.3 Relationship between geographic range within Britain (occupancy of 10 km squares in 1981/82 – 1983/84 – from Lack 1986) and the proportion of winter total in Britain contained within SPA suite within Britain for Annex I wintering waterbirds. [Logarithmic relationship: $y = -0.1744\mathrm{Ln}(x) + 1.4104$; $R^2 = 0.3818$]

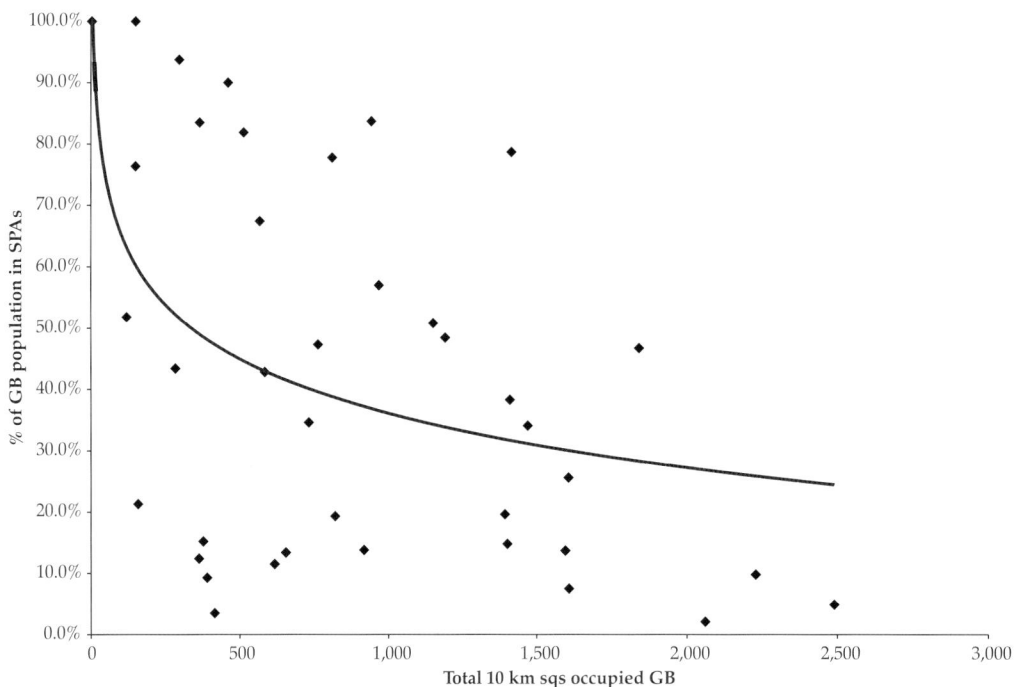

Figure 5.4 Relationship between geographic range within Britain (occupancy of 10 km squares in 1981/82 – 1983/84 – from Lack 1986) and the proportion of winter total in Britain contained within SPA suite within Britain for non-Annex I wintering waterbirds. [Logarithmic relationship: $y = -0.1277\mathrm{Ln}(x) + 1.2433$; $R^2 = 0.2222$]

populations are contained within UK SPAs respectively. This is because both are birds of the open, non-estuarine shoreline, occurring widely around the coasts of Britain, often at low densities. Where notable concentrations occur, these have been selected as SPAs (see species accounts A6.77 and A6.59b), but elsewhere their wide occurrence in low densities has prevented the identification of key sites.

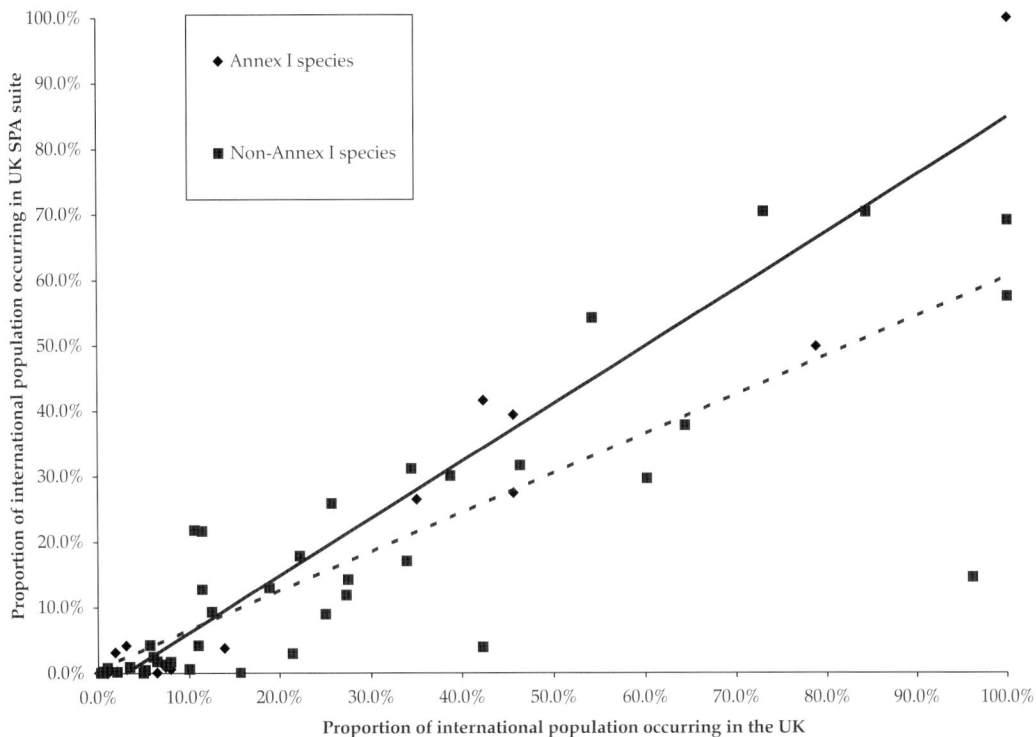

Figure 5.5 Proportionate inclusion of international populations of wintering waterbirds within the UK SPA network related to the proportion of those populations that winter in the UK. [Linear relationship from Annex I species: $y = 0.8743x - 0.0261$; $R^2 = 0.9353$. Linear relationship from migratory non-Annex I species: $y = 0.6018x + 0.0044$; $R^2 = 0.7029$]

It is also notable in Figure 5.5 that the slope of the relationship is steeper for Annex I species than for non-Annex I migratory species. This implies that, on average, for any international population present in the UK, a higher proportion of that population will be contained within the SPA network if the species (or sub-species) is listed on Annex I.

The selection of SPAs by the UK does thus reflect the concept of proportionate international responsibility.

6 Wider countryside conservation measures

6.1 The necessary mix of conservation measures: protected sites and wider measures

In the face of increasing human pressure on the natural environment, there are strong biological grounds to establish national and international networks of protected areas. A mixture of site-based and wider policies is essential, however, to meet the conservation requirements of most species. The following diagram illustrates this point. Each species will occur in a different place along the horizontal axis, with a different ideal mix of site-related and wider countryside conservation measures.

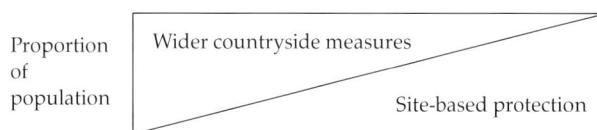

Other than for a few highly gregarious species, or birds with very small populations, the protection of selected sites alone is normally inadequate to conserve populations in the long term. The appropriate management of areas outside protected sites is also required. For broadly dispersed migratory species (such as Skylark, Fieldfare, Redwing and Willow Warbler) appropriate conservation measures are undertaken through policies addressed at the 'wider countryside'.

Bird populations within protected areas are frequently influenced by the consequences of land use in surrounding areas, and thus, protected sites are not closed units (Helle 1986; Janzen 1983; Schafer 1990). This highlights the need for taking a species-based approach to the provision of conservation needs, reviewing provision of both sites and complementary wider countryside needs. Section 4 explains how this has been undertaken in the UK in the context of this review.

6.2 Wider measures for birds in the UK

A variety of measures are in place for the conservation of birds away from protected sites. Some address specific needs of individual species and these are usually noted in the relevant species accounts.

Examples of such focused measures include:

● incentives for Corncrake-friendly farming in Scotland and Northern Ireland (species account A6.54);

● incentives for appropriate management of agricultural land for wintering geese in Scotland, especially Greenland Barnacle Goose on Islay, Orkney and the Solway Firth (A6.22), and for Greenland White-fronted Goose on Islay (A6.20);

● restoration, management and recreation of reed-swamps for Bitterns (A6.13);

Table 6.1 National (UK) biodiversity action or management plans for birds

Species	Species status		UK Biodiversity Steering Group Action Plan
	Annex I species	**UK migratory species**	
Bittern	✓	✓	✓
Common Scoter		✓ partial	✓
Black Grouse			✓
Capercaillie	✓		✓
Black Grouse			✓
Grey Partridge			✓
Corncrake	✓	✓	✓
Stone Curlew	✓	✓	✓
Red-necked Phalarope	✓	✓	✓
Roseate Tern	✓	✓	✓
Turtle Dove		✓	✓
Nightjar	✓	✓	✓
Wryneck		✓	✓
Woodlark	✓	✓ partial	✓
Skylark		✓ partial	✓
Song Thrush		✓ partial	✓
Aquatic Warbler	✓	✓	✓
Spotted Flycatcher		✓	✓
Red-backed Shrike	✓	✓	✓
Tree Sparrow			✓
Linnet		✓ partial	✓
Scottish Crossbill	✓		✓
Bullfinch			✓
Cirl Bunting			✓
Reed Bunting		✓ partial	✓

- various measures to reverse the decline of Capercaillie in Scotland, in particular addressing the issue of mortality as a result of collisions with deer-fencing (A6.52);

- peatland management for wader populations and their habitat in the Isle of Lewis;

- measures to reduce Stone Curlew mortality from agricultural operations within their core range (A6.58); and

- the establishment of national Biodiversity Action Plans for many species (Table 6.1).

Additionally, there are a range of schemes operative in the UK which have direct positive benefits for the conservation of birds. They include:

- various agri-environment schemes such as Tir Gofal in Wales, the Countryside Premium Scheme in Scotland and Countryside Stewardship in England, as well as Environmentally Sensitive Areas located throughout the UK;

- schemes operated by the country conservation agencies to improve the quality of habitat management within SSSIs, such as the Wildlife Enhancement Scheme in England;

- implementation of Regional Indicative Forestry Strategies, and other measures (Stroud 1998), in Scotland to steer new afforestation away from areas of high nature conservation sensitivity;

- implementation of Water-table Management Plans to address the issue of hydrological management of key wetland protected sites (in the context of wider needs for water in surrounding areas). These plans directly benefit a range of breeding and wintering waterbirds through maintaining high-quality wetland habitats (see Bientema *et al.* 1996 for review);

- implementation of a range of Estuary Management Plans and related initiatives for major estuaries throughout the UK. These assist in reducing conflicting demands on estuaries and related coastal habitats through encouragement of joint planning between the various users and other stakeholder groups (including the many agencies and departments with statutory responsibilities in these areas);

- introduction of legislation in England[1] in 1999 to outlaw the use of toxic lead gunshot for shooting of wildfowl quarry species as well as on SSSIs notified for their importance for waterbirds. Public consultation on similar measures in Scotland is currently underway. Consultation on a draft Statutory Instrument and Regulatory Appraisal is expected to take place in Wales in spring 2001;

- annual monitoring of the severity of winter weather which may lead to the temporary cessation of shooting in order to reduce mortality of quarry and non-quarry waterbirds in periods of great energetic stress (J. Stroud 1992); and

- establishment of processes that will lead to the creation and restoration of a range of threatened habitats under the UK's Biodiversity Action Plan (Biodiversity Steering Group 1995).

---

1 The Environmental Protection (Restriction on Use of Lead Shot) (England) Regulations 1999

7 Acknowledgements

The publication of this review is the conclusion of a major project, involving many organisations and individuals and undertaken over a protracted period – a consequence of its size and technical complexity. Initial work, commencing in 1993, focused on the derivation of selection guidelines for UK SPAs. These were published by JNCC in June 1999. Following on from this, work in 1998–2001 focused on the application of these guidelines to derive lists of qualifying sites and species (and completing the documentation presented here). We list below all those who have been involved in both phases of this activity (with apologies to anyone we have inadvertently omitted).

Work to derive site selection guidelines involved large numbers of individuals in the country agencies, organised as an Inter-Agency Working Group. Between 1993 and 1998, this involved: Michael Usher, Joyce Tait, Colin Galbraith, Mike Shepherd, Stephen Ward, Greg Mudge, Andy Douse and Nigel Buxton (for **SNH**); Malcolm Smith, Steve Parr and Peter Stuttard (for **CCW**), Keith Duff, John Finnie, Andy F. Brown, Pat Doody, Sue Collins, Alastair Burn, Dawn Isaac and Peter Clement (for **EN**), and Joe Furphy, Howard Platt and Richard Weyl (for the **Department of the Environment for Northern Ireland**); and Colin Galbraith, Alan Law, Mark Tasker and David Stroud. The later stages were guided by Roy Bunce, Graham Donald, Hilary Neal and Phil Lewis (**Department of the Environment**), Derek Beames, Jon Young and Richard Thomas (**Welsh Office**); and John Gilmour, John Davidson and John Miles (**Scottish Office**). This activity was lead by **JNCC** – principally by Colin Galbraith, with assistance from Alan Law, David Stroud, Roy Walker and Andy E. Brown.

Guidance through the site review (1998–2001) was provided by a Project Steering Group comprising: Phil Lewis, Hilary Neal, Nicola Donlon, John Miles, Jon Young, Peter Stuttard, Nigel Buxton, Peter Clement, Deryck Steer (chair 1998–1999), Ian McLean (chair 1999–2001), Steve Cook, Sarah Brocklehurst, David Stroud, Kathryn Farrell, Cameron Easton, Siân Whitehead, Trevor Salmon, Ian Bainbridge, Helen Baker, Ben Fraser and Christine Todd. Overall project management for JNCC was undertaken by Colin Galbraith (1993–1997), Andy E. Brown (1997–1998) and Ian McLean (1998–2001).

Day to day co-ordination within JNCC was undertaken by a number of SPA project officers: Alan Law (1993–1996), David Stroud (1996–1998, 1999, 2000–2001), Steve Cook (1998–1999), Sarah Brocklehurst (1999–2000) and Helen Baker (2001). The review would not have been possible without the skilled inputs of Dave Chambers, David Cole, Steve Cook, Brian Miller (GIS mapping), and Jason Reynolds who developed and maintained the necessary JNCC information and data management systems. General administrative support to the project officers and Steering Group was cheerfully provided by Ricky Mexson, Joanne Day, Cathy Gardner and Paul Fone.

The initial technical workshops to review species conservation needs and assess qualifying sites were attended by Nigel Buxton, Steve Cook, Siân Whitehead, Ross Johnston, David Stroud, Andy F. Brown, Phil Grice, Peter Clement, Mark Tasker, Kate Thompson, Helen Riley and Des Thompson.

Species and site accounts have been authored by a range of individuals both in the statutory agencies and in other organisations under contract: **SNH:** Nigel Buxton, Ross Johnston, Helen Baker, Phil Whitfield and Helen Riley; **JNCC:** David Stroud, Steve Cook, Sarah Brocklehurst, Mark Tasker, Nick Hodgetts and Ian McLean; **CCW:** Siân Whitehead; **EN:** Allan Drewitt, Ben Fraser, Andy F. Brown, Peter Clement and Richard Saunders; **Just Ecology:** Jeff Kirby, Rodney West and Malcolm Ogilvie; **WWT:** James Robinson and Seb Buckton, **BTO:** Nigel Burton, Rick Woodburn and Nigel Clark.

Data from BTO, WeBS and WWT databases were ably extracted by Peter Cranswick, Mark Pollitt and particularly by Colette Hall who responded to large and complex requests for data over an extended period.

We are grateful to the following for the provision of comments on draft texts and other supplementary data and information: **SNH:** Nigel Buxton, Helen Baker, Phil Whitfield, Helen Riley, Tim Dawson, Sally Blyth, Tony Mainwood, John Gibson, Jon Warren, Erica Knott, David MacArthur, Karen Osborn, David Bale, Dominic Sargent, Ian Jardine and Michael Usher; **CCW:** Siân Whitehead, Mary Roddick and Alan Hale; **EN:** Allan Drewitt, Ben Fraser and Peter Clement; **BTO:** Chris Wernham, Nigel Clark and Mike Blair; **National Assembly of Wales:** Jon Young; **Scottish Executive:** Cameron Easton, John Miles and Kathryn Farrell; **Department of the Environment, Transport and the Regions:** Phil Lewis; Northern Ireland **Environment and Heritage Service:** Richard Weyl; **European Commission:** Micheal Ó Briain. Throughout the review, English Nature's library staff cheerfully supplied literature and sought other relevant information.

During the consultation phase, comments and other input were co-ordinated by Duncan Huggett for **RSPB**; David Burges (WWF-UK) for **Wildlife and Countryside Link**; Jen Anderson for **Scottish Wildlife and Countryside Link**; and James Robinson for the **Wildfowl and Wetlands Trust**.

Detailed comments on the text of the draft SPA guidelines and/or this review were provided by the following: **RSPB:** David Pritchard, Duncan Huggett, Clifton Bain, Lloyd Austin, Tony Prater, Rowena Langston, Michael John Austin, Brian Etheridge, Gillian Gilbert, Murray Grant, David Hoccom, Julian Hughes, Digger Jackson, Kenny Kortland, Peter Newbery, Mark O'Brien, Duncan Orr-Ewing, James Pearce-Higgins, Ian Johnstone, Norman Ratcliffe, Graham Rebecca, Innes Sim, Ron Summers, Andy Tharme, Gwyn Williams and Robin Wynde; **WWF:** Rebecca May and David Burges; and **WWT:** James Robinson and Melanie Kershaw.

Publication arrangements for JNCC were overseen by Trudi Harris. Tim Davis and Tim Jones of DJEnvironmental skilfully copy-edited the entire document. The cover was designed by Cottier Sidaway from a concept by Helen Baker. Cover photographs are as follows: Cairngorms SPA, Scottish Natural Heritage; Light-bellied Brent Geese, David Tipling/Windrush; The Wash SPA, Peter Wakely; Knot, Chris Gomersall; Chough, Chris Gomersall; Glannau Ynys Gybi / Holy Island Coast SPA, Peter Wakely; Strangford Lough SPA, Mike Hartwell; Scottish Crossbill, Mike Read.

And finally, but by no means least, we are grateful to the very many thousands of volunteer birdwatchers throughout the UK who have contributed their time and information to organised monitoring schemes such as the Wetland Bird Survey and Breeding Bird Survey, or to the work of special interest groups such as the Raptor Study Groups. This review has sought to organise and review these data, and so to ensure that national conservation policies are developed based on the best available information. Needless to say, such a detailed review would not have been possible without these inputs. Monitoring the efficacy of the UK's SPA network in the long term will require sustained inputs. Thank you and please keep counting!

8 References

Adriaensen, F., Ulenaers, P. & Dhont, A.A. 1993. Ringing recoveries and the increase in numbers of European Great Crested Grebes *Podiceps cristatus*. *Ardea* 81: 59–70.

Aguilar, J.S. & Fernández, G. 2000. Species Action Plan for the Mediterranean Shag *Phalacrocorax aristotelis desmarestii* in Europe. Action Plan prepared by BirdLife International on behalf of the European Commission. 23 pp. Brussels.

Alexander, I. & Cresswell, B. 1990. Foraging by Nightjars *Caprimulgus europaeus* away from their nesting areas. *Ibis* 132: 568–574.

Alexander, W.B. & Lack, D. 1944. Changes in status among British breeding birds. *British Birds* 38: 42–45, 62–69, 82–88.

Allport, G. 1989a. *The effect of grazing on the distribution and feeding efficiency of the western taiga bean goose* Anser fabalis *in the Yare Valley*. PhD thesis, University of East Anglia.

Allport, G. 1989b. Norfolk's Bean Geese and their management. *RSPB Conservation Review* 3: 59–60.

Anderson, P. & Yalden, D.W. 1981. Increasing sheep numbers and the loss of heather moorland in the Peak District, England. *Biological Conservation* 20: 195–213.

Andrew, M. & Baines, D. 1997. The impact of deer fences on woodland grouse. *Report to Scottish Natural Heritage, Millennium Forest for Scotland Trust and the Royal Society for the Protection of Birds.* Newtonmore: Game Conservancy Trust.

Andrews, D.J., Mathers, R.G. & Rainey, E. 1996. Brent Geese feeding on agricultural land around Strangford Lough, Co. Down. *Irish Birds* 5: 407–412.

Andriesen, F., Ulenaers, P. & Dhont, A.A. 1993. Ringing recoveries and the increase in numbers of European Great Crested Grebes *Podiceps cristatus*. *Ardea* 81: 59–70.

Anker-Nilssen, T. & Barrett R.T. 1991. Status of seabirds in northern Norway. *British Birds* 84: 329–341.

Anonymous 1999. *Draft International Action Plan for the Dark-bellied Brent Goose.* Paper MoP1.15. Submitted to the First Meeting of Parties to the African Eurasian Waterbird Agreement, Cape Town, South Africa, November 1999. 47 pp.

Aplin, O.V. 1902. The birds of Bardsey Island, with additional notes on the birds of Lleyn, 2 parts. *The Zoologist* 5: 8–17, 107–110.

Armstrong, E.A. 1955. *The Wren.* London, Collins New Naturalist.

Aspinall, S.J. 1988. Fluctuating fortunes of the Fair Isle wren. *Fair Isle Bird Observatory Annual Report* 1987: 46–47.

Aspinall, S.J. & Dennis, R.H. 1988. Goosanders and Red-breasted Mergansers in the Moray Firth. *Scottish Birds* 15: 65–70.

Atkinson, N.K., Davies, M. & Prater, A.J. 1978. The winter distribution of Purple Sandpipers in Britain. *Bird Study* 25: 223–228.

Atkinson, P.W. 1996. The origins, moult, movements and changes in numbers of Bar-tailed Godwits *Limosa lapponica* on the Wash, England. *Bird Study* 43: 60–72.

Atkinson, R. & Ainslie, J.A. 1940. The British breeding status of Leach's Fork-tailed Petrel. *British Birds* 34: 50–55.

Atkinson-Willes, G.L. 1976. The numerical distribution of ducks, swans and coots as a guide in assessing the importance of wetlands in midwinter. In: *Proceedings of the international conference on the conservation of wetlands and waterfowl, 2–6 December 1974*, 199–254. Heiligenhafen, Federal Republic of Germany.

Atkinson-Willes, G.L. (ed.) 1963. *Wildfowl in Great Britain. A survey of the winter distribution of the Anatidae and their conservation in England, Scotland and Wales.* Monographs of the Nature Conservancy No. 3. London, HMSO. 368 pp.

Atkinson-Willes, G.L., Scott, D.A. & Prater, A.J. 1982. Criteria for selecting wetlands of international importance. In: *Proceedings of the conference on the conservation of wetlands of international importance especially as waterfowl habitat. Cagliari, Italy, 24–29 November 1980*, pp. 1017–1042. Supplemento alle Ricerche di Biologia della Selvaggina, 81 (1).

Aubrecht, G., Leuzinger, H., Schiffereli, L. & Schuster, S. 1990. Starker Einflug von Samtenten *Melanitta fusca* ins mitteleuropäische Binnenland in den Wintern 1985/86 und 1988/89. *Ornithologische Beobachter* 87: 89–97.

Austin, G.E., Peachel, I. & Rehfisch, M.M. 2000. Regional trends in coastal wintering waders in Britain. *Bird Study* 47: 352–371.

Avery, M. & del Nevo, A. 1991. Action for Roseate Terns. *RSPB Conservation Review* 5: 54–59.

Avery, M.I. & Haines-Young, R.H. 1990. Population estimates for the Dunlin *Calidris alpina* derived from remotely sensed satellite imagery of the Flow Country of northern Scotland. *Nature* 344: 860–862.

Avery, M.I., Burges, D., Dymond, N.J. & Ellis, P.M. 1993. The status of Arctic Terns *Sterna paradisaea* in Orkney and Shetland in 1989. *Seabird* 15: 17–19.

Baillie, S.R. 1986. Eider *Somateria mollissima*. In: *The Atlas of Wintering Birds in Britain and Ireland*. ed. Lack, P., pp. 114–115. Calton, T. & A.D. Poyser.

Baillie, S.R. & Milne, H. 1989. Movement of Eiders *Somateria mollissima* on the east coast of Britain. *Ibis* 131: 321–335.

Bainbridge I.P. & Minton, C.D.T. 1978. The migration and mortality of the Curlew in Britain and Ireland. *Bird Study* 25: 39–50.

Baines, D. & Summers, R.W. 1997. Assessment of bird collisions with deer fences in Scottish forests. *Journal of Applied Ecology* 34: 941–948.

Balfour, E. 1968. Breeding birds of Orkney. *Scottish Birds* 5: 89–104.

Barrett, J. & Barrett, C.F. 1985. Divers in the Moray Firth, Scotland. *Scottish Birds* 13: 149–154.

Batten, L.A., Bibby, C.J., Clement, P., Elliott, G.D. & Porter, R.F. (eds.) 1990. *Red Data Birds in Britain: action for rare, threatened and important species*. London, T. & A.D. Poyser.

Baxter, E.V. & Rintoul, L.J. 1953. *The birds of Scotland: their history, distribution and migration*. Edinburgh, Oliver & Boyd.

Beatty, J. 1992. *Sula: the seabird-hunters of Lewis*. London, Michael Joseph.

Beekman, J.H. 1997. International censuses of the northwest European Bewick's Swan population, January 1990 and 1995. *Swan Specialist Group Newsletter* 6: 7–9.

Beintema, A.J. & Müskens, G.J.D.M. 1983. Changes in migration pattern of the Common Snipe. In: *Proceedings of the 2nd European Woodcock and Snipe Workshop, 1982*, ed. by H. Kalchreuter. Fordingbridge. pp. 146–160.

Beintema, A.J., Dunn, E. & Stroud, D.A. 1996. Birds and wet grasslands. In: *Farming and birds in Europe: the Common Agricultural Policy and its implications for bird conservation*, ed. by D.J. Pain & M.W. Pienkowski. London, Academic Press. pp. 269–296.

Benn, S., Murray, S. & Tasker, M.L. 1989. *The birds of North Rona and Sula Sgeir*. Peterborough, Nature Conservancy Council.

Berg, Å. 1992. Factors affecting nest-site choice and reproductive success of curlews *Numenius arquata* on farmland. *Ibis* 134: 44–51.

Bergh, L. van den. 1999. Tundra Bean Goose *Anser fabalis rossicus*. In: *Goose populations of the Western Palearctic: a review of status and distribution*, by J. Madsen, G. Cracknell & A.D. Fox. Denmark, Wetlands International Publication No. 48/NERI. pp. 38–66.

Berndt, R.K. & Hario, M. 1997. Velvet Scoter *Melanitta fusca*. In: *The EBCC Atlas of European Breeding Birds: Their Distribution and Abundance*, ed. by W.J.M. Hagemeijer & M.J. Blair. London, T. & A.D. Poyser. pp. 117–118.

Berndt, R.K. & Hill, D. 1997. Mallard *Anas platyrhynchos*. In: *The EBCC Atlas of European Breeding Birds: Their Distribution and Abundance*, ed. by W.J.M. Hagemeijer & M.J. Blair. London, T. & A.D. Poyser. pp. 92–93.

Berndt, R.K. & Kauppinen, J. 1997. Pintail *Anas acuta*. In: *The EBCC Atlas of European Breeding Birds: Their Distribution and Abundance*, ed. by W.J.M. Hagemeijer & M.J. Blair. London, T. & A.D. Poyser. pp. 94–95.

Berndt, R.K. & Skov, H. 1997. Long-tailed Duck *Clangula hyemalis*. In: *The EBCC Atlas of European Breeding Birds: Their Distribution and Abundance*, ed. by W.J.M. Hagemeijer & M.J. Blair. London, T. & A.D. Poyser. p.115.

Berrow, S.D., Mackie, K.L., O'Sullivan, O., Shepherd, K.B., Mellon, C. & Coveney, J.A. 1993. The second international Chough survey in Ireland, 1992. *Irish Birds* 5: 1–10.

Berry, J. 1936. British mammals and birds as enemies of the Atlantic salmon *Salmo salar*. *Avon Biological Research, Annual Report 1934–35*: 31–36.

Berry, R.J. 1985. *The Natural History of Shetland*. New Naturalist No. 70. London, Collins.

Berry, J. 1939. *The status and distribution of wild geese and wild duck in Scotland*. Cambridge, University Press.

Bibby, C.J. 1979. Mortality and movements of Dartford Warblers in England. *British Birds* 72: 10–22.

Bibby, C.J. 1981. Wintering Bitterns in Britain. *British Birds* 74: 1–10.

Bibby, C.J. 1986. Merlins in Wales, site occupancy and breeding in relation to vegetation. *Journal of Applied Ecology* 23: 1–12.

Bibby, C.J. & Etheridge, B. 1993. Status of the Hen Harrier in Scotland in 1988–1989. *Bird Study* 40: 1–11.

Biber, J.-P. & Salathé, T. 1991. Threats to migratory birds. In: *Conserving migratory birds.* ICBP Technical Publication No. 12. Cambridge, ICBP. pp. 17–35.

Bignal, E.M. & Bignal, S. 1987. The provision of nesting sites for choughs. *Chief Scientist Directorate Report* No. 765. Peterborough , Nature Conservancy Council.

Bignal, E.M. & Curtis, D.J. eds. 1988. *Choughs and Land-use in Europe. Proceedings of an International Workshop on the Conservation of the Chough,* Pyrrhocorax pyrrhocorax, *in the EC. 11–14 November 1988.* Argyll, Scottish Chough Study Group.

Bignal, E.M. & McCracken, D.I. 1996. Low-intensity farming systems in the conservation of the countryside. *Journal of Applied Ecology* 33: 413–424.

Bignal, E.M., Bignal, S. & Curtis, D.J. 1989. Functional unit systems and support ground for choughs – the nature conservation requirements. In: *Choughs and Land-use in Europe,* ed. by E.M. Bignal & D.J. Curtis. Tarbert, Scottish Chough Study Group & Nature Conservancy Council. pp. 102–109.

Bignal, E.M., Bignal, S. & McCracken, D. 1997. The social life of the Chough. *British Wildlife* 8(6): 373–383.

Bignal, E.M., Curtis, D.J. & Matthews, J.L. 1988. *Islay: land types, bird habitats and nature conservation. Part 1: land use and birds on Islay.* Nature Conservancy Council Chief Scientist Directorate Report No. 809, Part 1. Peterborough.

Biodiversity Steering Group 1995. *Biodiversity: the UK Steering Group report.* Two volumes. London, HMSO. 324 pp.

Biodiversity Steering Group 1998. *UK Biodiversity Group. Tranche 2: Action Plans. Volume 1 – vertebrates and vascular plants.* London, HMSO. 267 pp.

Birkin, M. & Smith, A. 1987. *Breeding birds, Isles of Scilly 1987.* Nature Conservancy Council Report, Taunton, SW England Region.

Black, J.M. 1998. *Conservation and management plan for the Svalbard population of barnacle geese.* DN-Rapport 1998/2, Norwegian Directorate for Nature Management.

Black, J.M. & Rees, E.C. 1984. The structure and behaviour of the Whooper Swan population wintering at Caerlaverock, Dumfries and Galloway, Scotland: an introductory study. *Wildfowl* 35: 21–36.

Black, J.M., Patterson, D., Shimmings, P. & Rees, E.C. 1999. Barnacle Geese on the Solway: 1990–1996. *Scottish Birds 20*: 63–72.

Boisseau, S. & Yalden, D.W. 1998. The former status of the Crane *Grus grus* in Britain. *Ibis* 140: 482–500.

Boobyer, G. 1992. Population trends of the Golden Plover *Pluvialis apricaria* in Britain. Peterborough, JNCC.

Booth, C., Cuthbert, M. & Reynolds, P. 1984. *The Birds of Orkney.* Kirkwall, Orkney Press.

BOURC 2000. British Ornithologists' Union Records Committee: 27th Report (October 2000). *Ibis* 143: 171–175.

Bourne, W.R.P., Smith, A.J.M. & Douse A. 1978. Gulls and terns nesting inland in north-east Scotland. *Scottish Birds* 10: 50–53.

Bourne, W.R.P., Mackrill, E.J., Peterson, A.M. & Yésou, P. 1988. The Yelkouan Shearwater *Puffinus (puffinus?) yelkouan. British Birds* 81: 306–319.

Bowden, C.G.R. & Green, R.E. 1994. *The ecology of Nightjars on pine plantations in Thetford forest.* Unpublished report to the RSPB, June 1994.

Boyd, H. 1957. The White-fronted Geese of England and Wales. *Wildfowl Trust Annual Report* 8: 80–84.

Boyd, H. 1959. Movements of marked sea and diving ducks in Europe in 1959–60. *Wildfowl Trust Annual Report* 10: 59–70.

Boyd, H. 1963. *Whooper Swans seen in aerial surveys in parts of Iceland in early July 1963.* Slimbridge, WWT unpublished report.

Boyd, H. 1968. Barnacle Geese in the west of Scotland, 1957–67. *Wildfowl* 19: 96–107.

Boyd, H. 1992. Arctic summer conditions and British Knot numbers: an exploratory analysis. *Wader Study Group Bulletin* 64, *Supplement*: 144–152.

Boyd, H. & Eltringham, S.K. 1962. The Whooper Swans in Great Britain. *Bird Study* 9: 217–241.

Boyd, H. & Ogilvie, M.A. 1961. The distribution of Mallard ringed in southern England. *Wildfowl Trust Annual Report* 12: 125–136

Bräger, S, Meißner, J. & Thiel, M. 1995. Temporal and spatial abundance of wintering Common Eider *Somateria mollissima*, Long-tailed Duck *Clangula hyemalis*, and Common Scoter *Melanitta nigra* in shallow water areas of the south-western Baltic Sea. *Ornis Fennica* 72: 19–28.

Brazil, M.A. & Kirk, J. 1981. *The current status of Whooper Swans in Great Britain and Ireland*. University of Stirling, unpublished report.

Briggs, K. 1983. The distribution and reproduction of Ringed Plovers breeding coastally and inland in north-west England. *Bird Study* 30: 222–228.

Brindley, E. Unpublished RSPB report. *Habitat requirements of aquatic warblers* Acrocephalus paludicola *on autumn migration through the UK.* Sandy, RSPB.

Brindley, E., Norris, K., Cook, T., Babbs, S., Forster Brown, C., Massey, P., Thompson, R. & Yaxley, R. 1998. The abundance and conservation status of Redshank *Tringa totanus* nesting on saltmarshes in Great Britain. *Biological Conservation* 86: 289–297.

Brindley, E., Mudge, G., Dymond, N., Lodge, C., Ribbands, B., Steele, D., Ellis, P., Meek, E., Suddaby, D. & Ratcliffe, N. 1999. The status of Arctic Terns *Sterna paradisaea* at Shetland and Orkney in 1994. *Atlantic Seabirds* 1: 135–143.

British Ornithologist's Union 1992. *Checklist of Birds of Britain and Ireland.* Sixth edition. Tring, BOU. 50 pp.

Brooke, M. 1990. *The Manx Shearwater.* London, T. & A.D. Poyser.

Brown, A.E., Burn, A.J., Hopkins, J.J. & Way, S.F. (eds.) 1997. *The Habitats Directive: selection of Special Areas of Conservation in the UK.* JNCC Report No. 270. 297 pp.

Brown, A.F. 1991. *An annotated bibliography of moorland breeding bird and breeding wader surveys, 1970–1990.* JNCC Report No. 8. 167 pp.

Brown, A. F. 1993. The status of Golden Plover (*Pluvialis apricaria*) in the South Pennines. *Bird Study* 40: 196–202.

Brown, A.F. & Bainbridge, I.P. 1995. Grouse moors and upland breeding birds. In: *Heaths and Moorland: cultural landscapes*, ed. by D.B.A. Thompson, A.J. Hester & M.B. Usher. Edinburgh, HMSO. pp 51–66.

Brown, L. 1976. *British birds of prey.* Glasgow, Collins.

Brown, P. & Waterston, G. 1962. *The return of the Osprey.* London, Collins.

Brown, R.G.B. & Nettleship, D.N. 1984. The seabirds of northeastern North America; their present status and conservation requirements. In: *Scientific studies during the 'Kurdistan' tanker incident: proceedings of a workshop*, ed. by J. Vandermeulen. Bedford Institute of Oceanography Report Series BI-R-80–3, Dartmouth, Nova Scotia.

Buckland, S.T., Bell, M.V. & Picozzi, N. 1990. *The Birds of North-East Scotland.* Aberdeen, North-East Scotland Bird Club. 473 pp.

Buckley, P.A. & Buckley, F.G. 1984. Seabirds of the north and middle Atlantic coasts of the United States: their status and conservation. In: *Status and conservation of the world's seabirds*, ed. by J.P. Croxall, P.G.H. Evans & R.W. Schreiber. Cambridge, ICBP Technical Publication No.2. pp. 101–133.

Bullock, I.D. & Gomersall, C.H. 1981. The breeding population of terns in Orkney and Shetland in 1980. *Bird Study* 28: 187–200.

Burger, J. & Gochfeld, M. 1991. Human activity influence and diurnal and nocturnal foraging of Sanderlings (*Calidris alba*). *Condor* 93: 259–265.

Burgess, N.D., Evans, C.E. & Sorensen, J. 1989. *The management of heathland for Nightjars at Minsmere, Suffolk.* RSPB Management Case Study, January 1989.

Burton, N.H.K. & Evans, P.R. 1997. Survival and winter site-fidelity of Turnstones *Arenaria interpres* and Purple Sandpipers *Calidris maritima* in northeast England. *Bird Study* 44: 35–44.

Burton, N.H.K., Evans, P.R. & Robinson, M.A. 1996. Effects on shorebird numbers of disturbance, the loss of a roost site and its replacement by an artificial island at Hartlepool, Cleveland. *Biological Conservation* 77: 193–201.

Buxton, N.E., Summers, R.W. & Nicoll, M. 1985. The populations and biometrics of Purple Sandpipers in the Outer Hebrides. *Ringing and Migration* 6: 87–92.

Buxton, N.E., Symonds, F. & Bregazzi, P.R. 1995. *The numbers and distribution of the native Greylag Goose (*Anser anser*) on the north Scottish mainland.* SNH Report.

Byrkjedal, I. & Thompson, D.B.A. 1998. *Tundra Plovers. The Eurasian, Pacific and American Golden Plovers and Grey Plover.* London, T. & A.D. Poyser. 422 pp.

Cabot, D. & West, B. 1983. Studies on the population of Barnacle Geese wintering on the Inishkea Islands, Co. Mayo. *Irish Birds* 2: 318–336.

Cadbury, C.J. 1980. The status and habitats of the Corncrake in Britain 1978–79. *Bird Study* 28: 203–218.

Cadbury, C.J. & Olney, P.J.S. 1978. Avocet population dynamics in England. *British Birds* 71: 102–121.

Cadbury, C.J., Hill, D., Partridge, J. & Sorensen, J. 1989. The history of the Avocet population and its management in England since recolonisation. *RSPB Conservation Review* 3: 9–13.

Callaghan, D.A., Kirby, J.S. & Hughes, B. 1997. The effects of waterfowl hunting on biodiversity: implications for sustainability. In: *Harvesting Wild Species*, ed. by C.H. Freese. London, Johns Hopkins University Press. pp. 507–574.

Camp, S. & Simmons, K.E.L. 1983. *Handbook of the birds of Europe, the Middle East and North Africa*. Oxford University Press, Oxford.

Campbell, L.H. 1978. Patterns of distribution and behaviour of flocks of seaducks wintering at Leith and Musselburgh, Scotland. *Biological Conservation* 14: 111–123.

Campbell, L.H. 1984. The impact of changes in sewage treatment on seaducks wintering in the Firth of Forth, Scotland. *Biological Conservation* 28: 173–180.

Campbell, L.H. 1986a. Goldeneye *Bucephala clangula*. In: *The Atlas of Wintering Birds in Britain and Ireland*, ed. by P. Lack. Calton, T. & A.D. Poyser. pp. 122–123.

Campbell, L.H. 1986b. Long-tailed Duck *Clangula hyemalis*. In: *The Atlas of Wintering Birds in Britain and Ireland*, ed. by P. Lack. Calton, T. & A.D. Poyser. pp. 116–117.

Campbell, L.H. 1986c. Scaup *Aythya marila*. In: *The Atlas of Wintering Birds in Britain and Ireland*, ed. by P Lack. Calton, T. & A.D. Poyser. pp. 112–113.

Campbell, L.H. 1986d. Velvet Scoter *Melanitta fusca*. In: *The Atlas of Wintering Birds in Britain and Ireland*, ed. by P Lack. Calton, T. & A.D. Poyser. pp. 120–121.

Campbell, L.H. & Talbot, T.R. 1987. Breeding status of Black-throated Divers in Scotland. *British Birds* 80: 1–8.

Campbell, L.H., Standring, K.T. & Cadbury, C.J. 1978. Firth of Forth Oil Pollution incident, February 1978. *Marine Pollution Bulletin*: 335–339.

Camphuysen, C.J., Calvo, B., Durinck, J., Ensor, K., Follestad, A., Furness, R.W., Garthe, S., Leaper, G., Skov, H., Tasker, M.L. & Winter C.J.N. 1995. *Consumption of discards by seabirds in the North Sea*. Texel, NIOZ-Rapport 1995–5.

Camphuysen, C.J., Ens, B.J., Heg, D., Hulscher, J.B., van der Meer, J. & Smit, C.J. 1996. Oystercatcher *Haematopus ostralegus* winter mortality in the Netherlands: the effect of severe weather and food supply. *Ardea* 84A: 469–492.

Carp, E. 1980. *Directory of Wetlands of International Importance in the Western Palearctic*. UNEP/IUCN, Gland, Switzerland. 506 pp.

Carter, I. & Burn, A. 2000. Problems with rodenticides: the threat to Red Kites and other wildlife. *British Wildlife* 11: 192–197.

Catchpole, C.K. & Phillips, J.F. 1992. Territory quality and reproductive success in the Dartford Warbler *Sylvia undata* in Dorset, England. *Biological Conservation* 61: 209–215.

Catt, D., Baines, D., Moss, R., Leakey, F. & Picozzi, N. 1994. *Abundance and distribution of Capercaillie in Scotland 1992–94*. Unpublished report to SNH and RSPB.

Catt, D.C., Baines, D., Picozzi, N., Moss, R. & Summers, R.W. 1998. Abundance and distribution of capercaillie *Tetrao urogallus* in Scotland 1992–1994. *Biological Conservation* 85: 257–267.

Cayford, J.T. & Waters, R.J. 1996. Population estimates for waders Charadrii wintering in Great Britain, 1987/88–1991/92. *Biological Conservation* 77: 7–17.

Chandler, R.J. 1981. Influxes into Britain and Ireland of Red-necked Grebes and other waterbirds during winter 1978/79. *British Birds* 74: 55–81.

Chandler, R.J. 1986. Red-breasted Merganser *Mergus serrator*. In: *The Atlas of Wintering Birds in Britain and Ireland*, ed. by P. Lack. Calton, T. & A.D. Poyser. pp. 126–127.

Clark, N.A. 1983 *The ecology of Dunlin (*Calidris alpina *L.) wintering on the Severn Estuary*. PhD Thesis, University of Edinburgh.

Clark, N.A. & Blair, M.J. 1999. *Supporting information for the UK review of Special Protection Areas*. Unpublished report from the British Trust for Ornithology to JNCC. 70 pp.

Clark, N.A., Turner, B.S. & Young, J.F. 1982. Spring passage of Sanderlings *Calidris alba* on the Solway Firth. *Wader Study Group Bulletin* 36: 10–11.

Clarke, R & Watson, D. 1990. The Hen Harrier Winter Roost Survey in Britain and Ireland. *Bird Study* 37: 84–100.

Clarke, R & Watson, D. 1997. The Hen Harrier Winter Roost Survey. Thirteen winters' data reveal serious declines. *The Raptor* 24: 41–45.

Clausen, P., Madsen, J., Percival, S.M., Anderson, G.Q.A., Koffijberg, K., Mehlum, F. & Vangeruwe, D. 1999. Light-bellied Brent Goose *Branta bernicla hrota*: Svalbard. pp. 312–327. In: *Goose populations of the Western Palearctic: a review of status and distribution*, by J. Madsen, G. Cracknell & A.D. Fox. Denmark, Wetlands International Publication No. 48/NERI.

Clausen, P., Madsen, J., Percival, S.M., O'Connor, D. & Anderson, G.Q.A. 1998. Population development and changes in winter site use by the Svalbard Light-bellied Brent Goose *Branta bernicla hrota* 1980–1994. *Biological Conservation* 84: 157–165.

Colhoun, K. 2000. *I-WeBS Report 1997–98: Results of the fourth winter of the Irish Wetland Bird Survey.* Dublin, BirdWatch Ireland.

Collar, N.J., Crosby, M.J. & Stattersfield, A.J. 1994. *Birds to Watch 2. The world list of threatened birds.* BirdLife Conservation Series No. 4, Cambridge. 407 pp.

Colston, P. & Burton, P. 1988. *A Field Guide to the waders of Britain and Europe with North Africa and the Middle East.* London, Hodder & Stoughton.

Combridge, P. & Parr, C. 1992. Influx of Little Egrets in Britain and Ireland in 1989. *British Birds* 85: 16–21.

Cook, A.S., O'Dowd, B. & Durdin, C. 1994. *Breeding Redshanks on Essex saltmarshes in 1993.* Sandy, RSPB.

Cook, A.S., O'Dowd, B. & Durdin, C. 1995. *Breeding Redshanks on the Wash in 1994.* Sandy, RSPB.

Cormack, D. & Lohoar, G. 1999. *Report on the investigation of breeding success of Schedule 1 birds on Orford Ness.* Norwich, National Trust.

Cottier, E.J. & Lea, D. 1969. Black-tailed godwits, ruffs and black terns breeding on the Ouse Washes. *British Birds* 62: 259–270.

Coulson, J.C. 1963. The status of the Kittiwake in the British Isles. *Bird Study* 10: 147–179.

Coulson, J.C. 1983. The changing status of the Kittiwake *Rissa tridactyla* in the British Isles, 1969–1979. *Bird Study* 30: 9–16.

Coulson, J.C., Potts, G.R., Deans, I.R. & Fraser, S.M. 1968. Exceptional mortality of Shags and other seabirds caused by paralytic shellfish poison. *British Birds* 61: 381–404.

Coulson, J.C. & Thomas, C.S. 1985. Changes in the biology of the Kittiwake *Rissa tridactyla*: a 31-year study of a breeding colony. *Journal of Animal Ecology* 54: 9–26.

Craik, J.C.A. 1995. Effects of North American mink on the breeding success of terns and smaller gulls in west Scotland. *Seabird* 17: 3–11.

Craik, M. 1997. Long-term effects of North American Mink *Mustela vison* on seabirds in western Scotland. *Bird Study* 44: 303–309.

Cramp, S. ed. 1985. *Handbook of the Birds of Europe, the Middle East and North Africa: the Birds of the Western Palearctic*, Volume 4. Oxford, Oxford University Press.

Cramp, S. ed. 1988. *Handbook of the Birds of Europe, the Middle East and North Africa: the Birds of the Western Palearctic*, Volume 5. Oxford, Oxford University Press.

Cramp, S. ed. 1992. *Handbook of the Birds of Europe, the Middle East and North Africa: the Birds of the Western Palearctic*, Volume 6. Oxford, Oxford University Press.

Cramp, S. & Perrins, C.M. eds. 1994. *Handbook of the Birds of Europe, the Middle East and North Africa: the Birds of the Western Palearctic*, Volume 8. Oxford, Oxford University Press

Cramp, S. & Simmons, K.E.L. eds. 1977. *Handbook of the Birds of Europe, the Middle East and North Africa: the Birds of the Western Palearctic*, Volume I. Oxford, Oxford University Press

Cramp, S. & Simmons, K.E.L. eds. 1980. *Handbook of the Birds of Europe, the Middle East and North Africa: the Birds of the Western Palearctic*, Volume 2. Oxford, Oxford University Press.

Cramp, S. & Simmons, K.E.L. eds. 1983. *Handbook of the Birds of Europe, the Middle East and North Africa: the Birds of the Western Palearctic*, Volume 3. Oxford, Oxford University Press.

Cramp, S., Bourne, W.R.P. & Saunders, D. 1974. *The seabirds of Britain and Ireland.* London, Collins.

Cranswick, P., Pollitt, M., Musgrove, A. & Hughes, B. 1999. *The Wetland Bird Survey 1997–98: Wildfowl and Wader Counts.* Slimbridge: BTO, WWT, RSPB & JNCC. 218 pp.

Cranswick, P.A., Bowler, J.M., Delany, S.N., Einarsson, O., Garðarsson, A., McElwaine, J.G., Merne, O.J., Rees, E.C. & Wells, J.H. 1997. Numbers of Whooper Swans *Cygnus cygnus* in Iceland, Ireland and Britain in January 1995: results of the international Whooper Swan census. *Wildfowl* 47: 17–30.

Cranswick, P.A., Kirby, J.S. & Waters, R.J. 1992. *Wildfowl and Wader Counts 1991–92.* Slimbridge, WWT. 109 pp.

Cranswick, P.A., Mitchell, C.R., Merne, O.J., Ogilvie, M.A., Kershaw, M., Delany, S.N., MacKay, M. & Lilley, R. in press. Status and distribution of the Greenland population of Barnacle Goose *Branta leucopsis* in Britain and Ireland, 1993 to 1999. *Wildfowl.*

Cranswick, P.A., Waters, R.J., Evans, J. & Pollitt, M. 1995. *The Wetland Bird Survey 1993–94: Wildfowl and Wader Counts.* Slimbridge: BTO, WWT, RSPB & JNCC. 168 pp.

Cranswick, P.A., Waters, R.J., Musgrove, A. & Pollitt, M. 1997. *The Wetland Bird Survey 1995–96: Wildfowl and Wader Counts.* Slimbridge: BTO, WWT, RSPB & JNCC. 165 pp.

Cresswell, B. & Alexander, I. 1992. Activity patterns of foraging Nightjars *Caprimulgus europaeus.* In: Priede, I.G. & Swift, M. 1992. *Wildlife telemetry: remote monitoring and tracking of animals.* Chichester, Ellis Horwood Ltd.

Crewe, M.D. 1994. *Suffolk Birds 1993.* Ipswich, Suffolk Naturalists' Society.

Crewe, M.D. 1998. *Suffolk Birds Volume 46.* Ipswich, Suffolk Naturalists' Society.

Crick, H.Q.P. & Ratcliffe, D.A. 1995. The Peregrine *Falco peregrinus* breeding population of the United Kingdom in 1991. *Bird Study* 42: 1–19.

Crick, H.Q.P. & Sparks, T.H. 1999. Climate change related to egg-laying trends. *Nature* 399: 423–434.

Crick, H.Q.P., Dudley, C., Glue, D.E. & Thomson, D.L. 1997. UK birds are laying eggs earlier. *Nature* 388: 526.

Crick, H.Q.P, Baillie, S.R., Balmer, D.E., Bashford, R.I., Beaven, L.P., Dudley, C., Glue, D.E., Gregory, R.D., Marchant, J.H., Peach, W.J. & Wilson, A.M. 1998. Breeding birds in the wider countryside: their conservation status (1972–1996). *BTO Research Report* No. 198. Thetford, BTO.

Crooke, C., Dennis, R., Harvey, M. & Summers, R.W. 1993. Population size and breeding success of Slavonian Grebes in Scotland. In: *Britain's Birds in 1990–1991: the conservation and monitoring review.* pp. 135–138. BTO/JNCC.

Danielsen, F., Skov, H. & Durinck, J. 1993. Estimates of the wintering population of Red-throated Divers *Gavia stellata* and Black-throated Diver *Gavia arctica* in northwest Europe. *Proceedings of the Seventh Nordic Congress of Ornithology, 1990*: 18–24.

Darling, F.F. 1940. *Island years.* London, Bell.

Davenport, D. 1982. Influxes into Britain of Hen Harriers, Long-eared Owls and Short-eared Owls in winter 1978/879. *British Birds* 75: 309–316.

Davidson, N.C. 1991. Breeding waders on British estuarine wet grasslands. In: *Waders breeding on wet grasslands. Wader Study Group Bulletin* 61, *Supplement.* pp. 36–41.

Davidson, N.C. 1998. Compiling estimates of East Atlantic flyway populations wintering in coastal Europe in the early 1990s: a summary of the 1996 WSG wader populations workshop. *Wader Study Group Bulletin* 86: 18–25.

Davidson, N.C. & Piersma, T. 1992. The migration of Knots: conservation needs and implications. *Wader Study Group Bulletin* 64, *Supplement*: 198–209.

Davidson, N.C. & Stroud, D.A. 1996. Conserving international coastal habitat networks on migratory waterfowl flyways. *Journal of Coastal Conservation* 2: 41–54.

Davidson, N.C. & Wilson, J.R. 1992. The migration system of European-wintering Knots *Calidris canutus islandica*. In: The Migration of Knots. *Wader Study Group Bulletin* 64, *Supplement:* 39–51.

Davidson, N.C., Stroud, D.A., Rothwell, P.I. & Pienkowski, M.W. 1998. Towards a flyway conservation strategy for waders. *International Wader Studies* 10: 24–44.

Davidson, N.C., Laffoley, D. d'A., Doody, J.P., Way, L.S., Gordon, J., Key, R., Pienkowski, M.W., Mitchell, R. & Duff, K.L. 1991. *Nature conservation and estuaries in Great Britain.* Peterborough, Nature Conservancy Council. 422 pp.

Davis, J.W.F. 1974. Herring Gull populations and Man. *Nature in Wales* 14: 85–90.

Day, J.C.U. & Wilson, J. 1978. Breeding Bitterns in Britain. *British Birds* 71: 285–300.

Debout, G., Røv, N. & Sellers, R.M. 1995. Status and population development of Cormorants *Phalacrocorax carbo carbo* breeding on the Atlantic coast of Europe. *Ardea* 83: 47–59.

Delany, S. 1993. Introduced and escaped geese in Britain in summer 1991. *British Birds* 86: 591–599.

Delany, S. 1996a. *I-WeBS Report 1994–95: Results from the first winter of the Irish Wetland Bird Survey.* Dublin, BirdWatch Ireland. 109 pp.

Delany, S. 1996b. *Irish Wetland Bird Survey, 1995/96. Results from the second winter of the Irish Wetland Bird Survey.* Dublin, BirdWatch Ireland. 157 pp.

Delany, S. & Ogilvie, M.A. 1994. *Greenland Barnacle Geese in Scotland, March 1994.* Report to JNCC. Slimbridge, WWT. 19 pp.

Delany, S., Reyes, C., Hubert, E., Pihl, S., Rees, E., Haanstra, L. & van Strien, A. 1999. *Results from the International Waterbird Census in the Western Palearctic and Southwest Asia 1995 and 1996.* Wetlands International Publication No. 54. Wageningen, The Netherlands. 178 pp.

Dennis, M.K. 1996. *Tetrad Atlas of the Breeding Birds of Essex.* Colchester, The Essex Birdwatching Society.

Dennis, R.H. 1983. Purple Sandpipers breeding in Scotland. *British Birds* 76: 563–566.

Dennis, R.H. 1987. Osprey recolonisation. *RSPB Conservation Review* 1: 88–90.

Dennis, R.H. 1993. Goldeneye *Bucephala clangula*. In: *The New Atlas of Breeding Birds in Britain and Ireland: 1988–1991.* Ed. by D.W. Gibbons, J.B. Reid & R.A. Chapman, pp 88–89. London, T. & A.D. Poyser.

Dennis, R.H. & Pöysä, H. 1997. Goldeneye *Bucephala clangula*. In: *The EBCC Atlas of European Breeding Birds: Their Distribution and Abundance*, ed. by W.J.M. Hagemeijer & M.J. Blair, pp. 120–121. London, T. & A.D. Poyser.

Dennis, R.H., Ellis, P.M., Broad, R.A. & Langslow, D.R. 1984. The status of the Golden Eagle in Britain. *British Birds* 77: 592–607.

DETR 1994. *PPG 9. Planning Policy Guidance: Nature Conservation.* 59 pp. London, HMSO.

DETR/JNCC Raptor Working Group 1998. *Raptor Working Group's progress report to Ministers.* Peterborough, DETR/JNCC. 90 pp.

DETR/JNCC Raptor Working Group 2000. *Report of the UK Raptor Working Group.* Peterborough, DETR/JNCC. 123 pp.

Devort, M. 1977. *The Common Snipe – elements for an action plan.* OMPO/CICB, France. 99 pp.

Dierschke, V. 1998. Site-fidelity and survival of Purple Sandpipers *Calidris maritima* at Helgoland (SE North Sea). *Ringing & Migration* 19: 41–48.

Dobbs, A. 1975. *The Birds of Nottinghamshire past and present.* Newton Abbot, David and Charles.

Dore, C. & Ellis, P.M. 1994. *An estimate of the population of Whimbrel* Numenius phaeopus *breeding in Shetland during 1989–1992 and a comparison with previous estimates.* Unpublished RSPB report.

Duncan, N. 1981. The Abbeystead and Mallowdale gull colonies before control. *Bird Study* 28: 133–138.

Dunn, E.H., Hussell, D.J.T. & Daniel, A. Welsh. 1999. Priority-setting tool applied to Canada's landbirds based on concern and responsibility for species. *Conservation Biology* 13: 1404–1415.

Dunn, R. 1837. *The Ornithologist's Guide to the Islands of Orkney & Shetland.* Hull. 128 pp.

Durinck, J., Christensen, K.D., Skov, H. & Danielsen, F. 1993. Diet of the Common Scoter *Melanitta nigra* and Velvet Scoter *M. fusca* wintering in the North Sea. *Ornis Fennica* 70: 215–218.

Durinck, J., Skov, H., Jensen, F.P. & Pihl, S. 1984. Important marine areas for wintering birds in the Baltic Sea, winter 1992. *Ornis Svecica* 3: 11–26.

Easterbee, N., Stroud, D.A., Bignal, E.M. & Dick, T.D. 1987. The arrival of Greenland Barnacle Geese at Loch Gruinart, Islay. *Scottish Birds* 14: 175–179.

Ebbinge, B.S. 1991. The impact of hunting on mortality rates and spatial distribution of geese wintering in the western Palearctic. *Ardea* 79: 197–209.

Ebbinge, B.S. 1992. Regulation of numbers of Dark-bellied Brent Geese *Branta bernicla bernicla* on spring staging sites. *Ardea* 80: 203–228.

Ebbinge, B.S. & St. Joseph, A.K.M. 1992. The Brent Goose Colour-ringing Scheme: unraveling annual migratory movements from high arctic Siberia to the coasts of western Europe. pp. 93–104. In: *Population limitation in Arctic -breeding Geese. Welke factoren beperken de populatie-grotte bij arctische ganzen?* by B.S. Ebbinge. PhD thesis, Riksuniversiteit Groningen, The Netherlands. 200 pp.

Ebbinge, B.S., Berrevoets, C., Clausen, P., Ganter, B., Günther, K., Koffiijberg, K., Mahéo, R., Rowcliffe, M., St. Joseph, A.K.M., Südbeck, P. & Syroechkovsky Jr., E.E. 1999. Dark-bellied Brent Goose *Branta bernicla bernicla.* In: In: *Goose populations of the Western Palearctic: a review of status and distribution,* by J. Madsen, G. Cracknell & A.D. Fox. Denmark, Wetlands International Publication No. 48/NERI. pp. 284–297.

Eerden, M.R. van & Gregersen, J. 1995. Long-term changes in the northwest European population of Cormorants *Phalacrocorax carbo sinensis. Ardea* 83: 61–79.

Engelmoer, M. & Roselaar, C. 1998. *Geographical variation in waders.* Kluwer, Dordrecht, The Netherlands. 305 pp.

Etheridge, B. in press. Hen Harrier *Circus cyaneus.* In: *The migration atlas: movements of the birds of Britain and Ireland,* by C.V. Wernham, M.P. Toms, J.H. Marchant, J.A. Clark, G.M. Siriwardena & S.R. Baillie. T. & A.D. Poyser, London.

Etheridge, B., Summers, R.W. & Green, R.E. 1997. The effects of illegal killing and destruction of nests by humans on population dynamics of the hen harrier *Circus cyaneus* in Scotland. *Journal of Applied Ecology* 34: 1081–1105.

European Commission 1991. *CORINE biotopes manual – a method to identify and describe consistently sites of major importance for nature conservation. Methodology – Volume 1.* Luxembourg, Office for Official Publications of the European Communities. 70 pp.

Evans, I.M. & Pienkowski, M.W. 1991. World status of the Red Kite. A background to the experimental reintroduction to England and Scotland. *British Birds* 84: 171–187.

Evans, I.M., Dennis, R.H., Orr-Ewing, D.C., Kjellén, N., Andersson, P.-O., Sylvén, M., Senosiain, A. & Carbo, F.C. 1997. The re-establishment of Red Kite breeding populations in Scotland and England. *British Birds* 90: 123–138.

Evans, I.M., Love, J.A., Galbraith, C.A. & Pienkowski, M.W. 1994. Population and range restoration of threatened raptors in the United Kingdom. In: *Raptor Conservation Today,* ed. by B.-U. Meyburg & R.D. Chancellor. World Working Group on Birds of Prey. Berlin, Pica Press. pp. 447–457.

Evans, I.M., Summers, R.W., O'Toole, L., Orr-Ewing, D.C., Evans, R. & Snell, N. 1999. Evaluating the success of translocating Red Kites *Milvus milvus* to the UK. *Bird Study* 46: 129–144.

Evans, P.R. 1981. Migration and dispersal of shorebirds as a survival strategy. In: *Feeding and survival strategies of estuarine organisms,* ed. by N.V. Jones & W.J. Wolff, pp. 275–290. New York, Plenum Press.

Evans, P.R. & Flower, W.U. 1967. The birds of the Small Isles. *Scottish Birds* 4: 404–445.

Evans, R.J. 2000. Wintering Slavonian Grebes in coastal waters of Britain and Ireland. *British Birds* 93: 218–226.

Everett, M.J. 1971. Breeding status of Red-necked Phalaropes in Britain and Ireland. *British Birds* 64: 293–302.

Everett, M.J. 1987. The Elmley experiment. *RSPB Conservation Review* 1: 31–33.

Everett, M.J., Hepburn, I.R., Ntiamoa-Baidu, Y. & Thomas, G.J. 1987. Roseate Terns in Britain and west Africa. *RSPB Conservation Review* 1: 56–58.

Ewins, P.J., Ellis, P.M., Bird, D.B. & Prior, A. 1988. The distribution and status of Arctic and Great Skuas in Shetland 1985–1986. *Scottish Birds* 15: 9–20.

Fair Isle Bird Observatory 1948–1999. *Annual report*. Fair Isle, Fair Isle Bird Observatory.

Ferns, P.N. 1980. The spring migration of Sanderlings *Calidris alba* through Britain in 1979. *Wader Study Group Bulletin* 30: 22–25.

Ferns, P.N. 1992. *Bird life of coasts and estuaries*. Cambridge, Cambridge University Press. 336 pp.

Ferns, P.N., Green, G.H. & Round, P.D. 1979. Significance of the Somerset and Gwent Levels in Britain as feeding areas for migrant Whimbrels *Numenius phaeopus*. *Biological Conservation* 16: 7–22.

Fisher, J. 1952. *The Fulmar*. London, Collins (New Naturalist Monographs, No. 6).

Fisher, J. & Vevers, H.G. 1943–44. The breeding distribution, history and population of the North Atlantic Gannet *Sula bassana*. *Journal of Animal Ecology* 12: 173–213; 13: 49–62.

Fleet, D.M., Frikke, J., Südbeck, P. & Vogel, R.L. 1994. Breeding birds in the Wadden Sea 1991. *Wadden Sea Ecosystem* No. 1. Wilhelmshaven, Common Wadden Sea Secretariat & Trilateral Monitoring and Assessment Group.

Flint, V.Y. & Krivenko, V.G. 1990. The present status and trends of waterfowl in the USSR. In: *Managing Waterfowl Populations*, ed. by G.V.T. Matthews, Proceedings of the IWRB Symposium Astrakhan 1989: 23–26. Slimbridge, IWRB Special Publication No. 12.

Fowler, J.A. 1982. Leach's Petrels present on Ramna Stacks, Shetland. *Seabird Report* 6: 93.

Fox, A.D. 1988. Breeding status of the Gadwall in Britain and Ireland. *British Birds* 81: 51–66.

Fox, A.D. 1991. The Gadwall in Britain. *British Wildlife* 91: 65–69.

Fox, A.D. 1994. Estuarine winter feeding patterns of Little Grebes *Tachybaptus ruficollis* in Central Wales. *Bird Study* 41: 15–24.

Fox, A.D. & Francis, I.S. 1998. *Report of the 1997/98 national census of Greenland White-fronted Geese in Britain*. GWGS report to WWT, Kalø, Denmark. 16 pp.

Fox, A.D. & Mitchell, C.R. 1988. Migration and seasonal distribution of Gadwall from Britain and Ireland: a preliminary assessment. *Wildfowl* 39: 145–152.

Fox, A.D. & Salmon, D.G. 1988. Changes in non-breeding distribution and habitat of Pochard *Aythya ferina* in Britain. *Biological Conservation* 46: 303–316.

Fox, A.D. & Salmon, D.G. 1989. The winter status and distribution of Gadwall in Britain and Ireland. *Bird Study* 36: 37–44

Fox, A.D. & Stawarczyk, T. 1997. Pochard *Aythya ferina*. In: *The EBCC Atlas of European Breeding Birds: Their Distribution and Abundance*, ed. by W.J.M. Hagemeijer & M.J. Blair. London, T. & A.D. Poyser. pp. 102–103.

Fox, A.D. & Stroud, D.A. 1985. The Greenland White-fronted Goose in Wales. *Nature in Wales, new series* 4: 20–27.

Fox, A.D. & Stroud, D.A. in press. *Anser albifrons flavirostris* Dalgety & Scott 1948, Greenland White-fronted Goose. *Birds of the Western Palearctic Update* .

Fox, A.D., Francis, I.S. & Stroud, D.A. 1989. Greenland white-fronted geese on Coll and Tiree: numbers, distribution and conservation. In: *The Birds of Coll and Tiree: status, habitat and conservation*, ed. by D.A. Stroud. Edinburgh, Nature Conservancy Council. pp. 129–142.

Fox, A.D., Gitay, H., Owen, M., Salmon, D.G. & Ogilvie M.A. 1989. Population dynamics of Icelandic-nesting geese, 1960–1987. *Ornis Scandinavica* 20: 289–297.

Fox, A.D., Hilmarsson, J.Ó., Einarsson, Ó., Boyd, H., Kristiansen, J.N., Stroud, D.A., Walsh, A.J., Mitchell, C., Francis, I.S. & Nygaard, T. 1999. Phenology and distribution of ringing recoveries and resightings of individually marked Greenland White-fronted Geese *Anser albifrons flavirostris* staging in Iceland. *Wildfowl* 50: 31–45.

Fox, A.D., Jarret, N., Gitay, H. & Paynter, D. 1989. Late summer habitat selection by breeding waterfowl in northern Scotland. *Wildfowl* 40: 106–114.

Fox, A.D., Mitchell, C., Stewart, A., Fletcher, J.D., Turner, J.V.N., Boyd, H., Salmon, D.G., Haines, W.G. & Tomlinson, C. 1994a. Winter movements and site fidelity of Pink-footed Geese *Anser brachyrhynchus* ringed in Britain, with particular emphasis on those marked in Lancashire. *Bird Study* 41: 221–234.

Fox, A.D., Norriss, D.W., Stroud, D.A. & Wilson, H.J. 1994b. Greenland White-fronted Geese in Ireland and Britain 1982/83–1993/94 – the first twelve years of international conservation monitoring. *Greenland White-fronted Goose Study Research Report No. 8.* Dublin, GWGS, Aberystwyth & National Parks and Wildlife Service. 55 pp.

Fox, A.D., Norriss, D.W., Stroud, D.A., Wilson, H.J. & Merne, O.J. 1998. The Greenland White-fronted Goose *Anser albifrons flavirostris* in Ireland and Britain 1982/83–1994/95: population change under conservation legislation. *Wildlife Biology* 4: 1–12.

Fox, A.D., Ogilvie, M.A., Easterbee, N. & Bignal, E.M. 1990. East Greenland Barnacle Geese in Scotland, spring 1988. *Scottish Birds* 16: 1–9.

Francis, I.S. & Thorpe, A. 1999. The breeding status of the Spotted Crake in north-east Scotland. *Scottish Birds* 20: 14–17.

Fraser, P.A., Lansdown, P.G. & Rogers, M.J. 1997. Report on scarce migrant birds in Britain in 1995. *British Birds* 90: 413–439.

Frederiksen, M., Fox, A.D., Madsen, J. & Colhoun, K. 2001. Estimating the total number of birds using a staging site. *Journal of Wildlife Management* 65(2): 282–289.

Fuller, R.J. 1978. Breeding populations of Ringed Plovers and Dunlins in the Uists and Benbecula, Outer Hebrides. *Bird Study* 25: 97–102.

Fuller, R.J. 1982. *Bird habitats in Britain.* Calton, T. & A.D. Poyser. 320 pp.

Fuller, R.J. & Gough, S. 1999. Changes in sheep numbers in Britain: implications for bird populations. *Biological Conservation* 91: 73–89.

Fuller, R.J. & Youngman, R.E. 1979. The utilisation of farmland by Golden Plovers wintering in southern England. *Bird Study* 26: 37–46.

Fuller, R.J. & Jackson, D.B. 1999. Changes in populations of breeding waders on the machair of North Uist, Scotland, 1983–1998. *Wader Study Group Bulletin* 90: 47–55.

Fuller, R.J., Reed, T.M., Buxton, N.E., Webb, A. Williams, T.D. & Pienkowski, M.W. 1986. Populations of breeding waders Charadrii and their habitats on the crofting lands of the Outer Hebrides, Scotland. *Biological Conservation* 37: 333–361.

Furness, R.W. 1981. Seabird populations on Foula. *Scottish Birds* 11: 237–253.

Furness, R.W. 1987. *The Skuas.* Calton, T. & A.D. Poyser.

Furness, R.W. 1997. Great Skua *Stercorarius skua.* In: *The EBCC Atlas of European Breeding Birds: Their Distribution and Abundance,* ed. by W.J.M. Hagemeijer & M.J. Blair. London, T. & A.D. Poyser.

Galbraith, C.A. 1992. *Mussel Farms: Their management alongside Eider ducks.* Edinburgh, Scottish Natural Heritage. 22 pp.

Galbraith, H., Murray, S., Duncan, K., Smith, R., Whitfield, D.P. & Thompson, D.B.A. 1993. Numbers and distribution of Dotterel *Charadrius morinellus* breeding in Great Britain. *Bird Study* 40: 161–169.

Garðarsson, A. 1991. Movements of Whooper Swans *Cygnus cygnus* neck-banded in Iceland. In: *Proceedings of the Third International Swan Symposium,* ed. by J. Kear, pp. 189–194. *Wildfowl* Supplement No. 1

Garðarsson, A. 1997. Whooper Swan *Cygnus cygnus.* In: *The EBCC Atlas of European Breeding Birds: Their Distribution and Abundance,* ed. by W.J.M. Hagemeijer & M.J. Blair. London, T. & A.D. Poyser. pp. 124–125.

Gibbons, D.W. & Wotton, S. 1996. The Dartford Warbler in the United Kingdom in 1994. *British Birds* 89: 203–212.

Gibbons, D.W., Bainbridge, I.P., Mudge, G.P., Tharme, A.P. & Ellis, P.M. 1997. The status and distribution of the Red-throated Diver *Gavia stellata* in Britain in 1994. *Bird Study* 44: 194–205.

Gibbons, D.W., Reid, J.B. & Chapman, R.A. 1993 *The New Atlas of Breeding Birds in Britain and Ireland: 1988–1991.* London, T. & A.D. Poyser. 520 pp.

Gilbert, G., Gibbons, D.W. & Evans, J. 1998. *Bird monitoring methods: a manual of techniques for key UK species.* Sandy: RSPB, BTO, WWT, JNCC, ITE and the Seabird Group. 464 pp.

Gilbert, G., Ruff, S., Tyler, G. & Smith, K. 1999. *Bittern* Botaurus stellaris *monitoring and research in the UK: summary of the 1999 season.* Unpublished report, RSPB, Sandy.

Gilburn, A.S. & Kirby, J.S. 1992. *Winter status, distribution and habitat use by Teal in the United Kingdom.* Slimbridge, WWT report to JNCC.

Gilpin, M. & Hanski, I. (eds.) 1991. *Metapopulation dynamics: empirical and theoretical investigations.* London, Academic Press. 336 pp.

Gittings, T. & Delany, S. 1996. A pre-breeding census of Common Scoters in Ireland in 1995. *Irish Birds* 5: 413–422.

Golovkin, A.N. 1984. Seabirds nesting in the USSR: the status and protection of populations, pp 473–486 In: *Status and conservation of the world's seabirds,* ed. by J.P Croxall, P.G.H. Evans & R.W. Shreiber, R.W. Cambridge, ICBP Technical Publication No. 2.

Gomersall, C.H. 1981. *Breeding Red-throated Divers in Shetland, 1981.* Unpublished report to RSPB.

Gomersall, C.H. 1982. *Breeding Red-throated Divers in Shetland, 1982.* Unpublished report to RSPB.

Gorban, I. & Stanevicius, V. 1997. Coot *Fulica atra.* In: *The EBCC Atlas of European Breeding Birds: Their Distribution and Abundance,* ed. by W.J.M. Hagemeijer & M.J. Blair. London, T. & A.D. Poyser. pp. 236–237.

Goss-Custard, J.D. & Moser, M.E. 1988. Rates of change in the number of Dunlin *Calidris alpina* wintering in British estuaries in relation to the spread of *Spartina anglica. Journal of Applied Ecology* 25: 95–109.

Goss-Custard, J.D., Ross, J., McGrorty, S., Durell, S.E.A. Le V. dit, Caldow, R.W.G. & West, A.D. 1998. Locally stable wintering numbers in the Oystercatcher *Haematopus ostralegus* where carrying capacity has not been reached. *Ibis* 140: 104–112.

Grant, J.R. & McGrady, M.J. 1999. Dispersal of Golden Eagles *Aquila chrysaetos* in Scotland. *Ringing & Migration* 19: 169–174.

Grant, M.C. 1998. Breeding curlews in the UK: RSPB research and implications for conservation. *RSPB Conservation Review* 11: 67–73.

Grant, M.C., Orsman, C., Easton, J., Lodge, C., Smith, M., Thompson, G., Rodwell, S. & Moore, N. 1999. Breeding success and causes of breeding failure of curlew *Numenius arquata* in Northern Ireland. *Journal of Applied Ecology* 36: 59–74.

Grant, M.E. 1991. Nesting densities, productivity and survival of breeding whimbrel *Numenius phaeopus* in Shetland. *Bird Study* 38: 160–169.

Grant, M.E. 1992. The effects of re-seeding heathland on breeding whimbrel in Shetland. I. Nest distributions. *Journal of Applied Ecology* 29: 501–508.

Grant, M.E., Chambers, R.E. & Evans, P.R. 1992a. The effects of re-seeding heathland on breeding whimbrel in Shetland. II. Habitat use by adults during pre-laying period. *Journal of Applied Ecology* 29: 509–515.

Grant, M.E., Chambers, R.E. & Evans, P.R. 1992b. The effects of re-seeding heathland on breeding whimbrel in Shetland. III. Habitat use by broods. *Journal of Applied Ecology* 29: 501–508.

Grant, P.J. & the British Birds Rarities Committee 1982. Rarities Committee news and announcements. *British Birds* 75: 337–338.

Green, G.P. 1981. *Dorset Bird Report 1980.* Dorchester, Dorset Natural History and Archaeological Society.

Green, R.E. 1995. The decline of the Corncrake *Crex crex* in Britain continues. *Bird Study* 42: 66–75.

Green, R.E. 1996. Factors affecting the population density of the Corncrake *Crex crex* in Britain and Ireland. *Journal of Applied Ecology* 33: 237–248.

Green, R.E. 1996. The status of the Golden Eagle in Britain in 1992. *Bird Study* 43: 20–27.

Green, R.E. & Gibbons, D.W. 2000. The status of the Corncrake *Crex crex* in Britain in 1998. *Bird Study* 47: 129–137.

Green, R.E. & Riley, H.T. 1999. *Corncrakes: Naturally Scottish.* Scottish Natural Heritage.

Green, R.E. & Robins, M. 1993. The decline of the ornithological importance of the Somerset Levels and Moors, England and changes in the management of water levels. *Biological Conservation* 66: 95–106.

Green, R.E., Cadbury, C.J. & Williams, G. 1987. Floods threaten Black-tailed Godwits breeding at the Ouse Washes. *RSPB Conservation Review* 1: 14–16.

Green, R.E., Rocamora, G. & Shäfer, N. 1997a. Populations, ecology and threats to the Corncrake *Crex crex* in Europe. *Vogelwelt* 118: 117–134.

Green, R.E., Tyler, G.A., Stowe, T.J. & Newton, A.V. 1997b. A simulation model of the effect of mowing of agricultural grassland on the breeding success of the Corncrake (*Crex crex*). *Journal of Zoology. London* 243: 81–115.

Greenwood, J.G. 1984. Migration of Dunlin *Calidris alpina*: a worldwide overview. *Ringing & Migration* 5: 35–39.

Gregory, M. 1996. Golden Eagles in south Argyll 1964–1995. *Argyll Bird Report* 12: 85–88.

Gregory, R.D., Carter, S.P. & Baillie, S.R. 1997. Abundance, distribution and habitat use of breeding Goosanders *Mergus merganser* and Red-breasted Mergansers *Mergus serrator* on British rivers. *Bird Study* 44: 1–12.

Gribble, F.C. 1976. A census of Black-headed Gull colonies. *Bird Study* 23: 135–145.

Gribble, F.C. 1983. Nightjars in Britain and Ireland in 1981. *Bird Study* 30: 165–176.

Griffin, B., Saxton, N. & Williams, I. 1991. *Breeding Redshanks in Wales, 1991.* Sandy, RSPB.

Grimmett, R.F.A. & Gammell, A.B. 1989. *Inventory of Important Bird Areas in the European Community.* Unpublished report prepared for the Directorate-General for the Environment, Consumer Protection and Nuclear Safety of the European Community, study contract B6610–54–88. ICBP, Cambridge, UK.

Grimmett, R.F.A. & Jones, T.A. 1989. *Important bird areas in Europe.* ICBP Technical Publication No. 9, Cambridge.

Gromadzka, J. 1998. Numbers of juvenile Dunlin *Calidris alpina* ringed at the Vistula Mouth (southern Baltic, Poland) in relation to Arctic breeding conditions. In: *Migration and international conservation of waders. Research and conservation on North Asian, African and European flyways,* ed. by H. Hötker, E. Lebedeva, P.S.

Tomkovich, J. Gromadzka, N.C. Davidson, J. Evans, D.A. Stroud & R.B. West. *International Wader Studies* 10: 85–87.

Gubbay, S. 1992. Progress and opportunities for advancing marine nature conservation through coastal zone management in the United Kingdom. *Aquatic Conservation: marine and freshwater ecosystems* 2: 357–362

Gudmundsson, G.A. & Lindström, T. 1992. Spring migration of Sanderlings *Calidris alba* through SW Iceland: where, from and to where? *Ardea* 80: 315–326.

Gurney, J.H. 1913. *The Gannet. A bird with a history.* London, Witherby.

Haapanen, A. 1991. Whooper swan *Cygnus c. cygnus* population dynamics in Finland. In: *Proceedings of the 3rd IWRB International Swan Symposium, Oxford, 1989*. ed. by J. Sears & P.J. Bacon. *Wildfowl, Supplement* 1: 137–141.

Hable, E. 1980. Beringungsergebnisse an der alpinen Population des Mornellregenpfeifers, *Eudromias morinellus* (L.). *Mitteilungen Abteilung für Zoologie und Botanik Landesmuseum "Johanneum"* 9: 81–85.

Hafner, H., Kayser, Y. & Pineau, O. 1994. Ecological determinants of annual fluctuations in numbers of breeding Little Egrets *Egretta garzetta* in the Camargue, S. France. *Revue Ecol. (Terre Vie)* 49: 53–62.

Hagemeijer, W.J.M. & Blair, M.J. (eds.) 1997. *The EBCC Atlas of European Breeding Birds: Their Distribution and Abundance.* London, T. & A.D. Poyser.

Haldin, M. 1997. Scaup *Aythya marila*. In: *The EBCC Atlas of European Breeding Birds: Their Distribution and Abundance*, ed. by W.J.M. Hagemeijer & M.J. Blair. London, T. & A.D. Poyser. pp. 108–109.

Halley, D.J. 1998. Golden and White-tailed Eagles in Scotland and Norway: coexistence, competition and environmental degradation. *British Birds* 91: 171–179.

Hamer, K.C., Furness, R.W. & Caldow, R.W.G. 1991. The effects of changes in food availability on the breeding ecology of Great Skuas, *Catharacta skua* in Shetland. *Journal of Zoology, London* 223: 175–188.

Hamer, K.C., Monaghan, P., Uttley, J.D., Walton, P. & Burns, M.D. 1993. The influence of food supply on the breeding ecology of Kittiwakes *Rissa tridactyla* in Shetland. *Ibis* 135: 255–263.

Hancock, M. 2000. Artificial floating island for nesting Black-throated Divers *Gavia arctica* in Scotland: construction, use and effect on breeding success. *Bird Study* 47(2): 165–175.

Hancock, M. & Avery, M.I. 1998. Changes in breeding bird populations in peatlands and young forestry in northeast Sutherland and Caithness between 1988 and 1995. *Scottish Birds* 19: 195–205.

Hancock, M.H., Gibbons, D.W. & Thompson, P.S. 1997. The status of the breeding Greenshank *Tringa nebularia* in the United Kingdom in 1995. *Bird Study* 44: 290–302.

Hardy, A.R. & Minton, C.D.T. 1980. Dunlin migration in Britain and Ireland. *Bird Study* 27: 81–92.

Hario, M. & Selin, K. 1988. Thirty-year trends in an Eider population: timing of breeding, clutch size, and nest site preferences. *Finnish Game Research* 45: 3–10.

Harris, M.P. 1966. Rates and causes of increases of some British gull populations. *Bird Study* 13: 84–95.

Harris, M.P. 1970. Rates and causes of increases of some British gull populations. *Bird Study* 17: 325–335.

Harris, M.P. 1984. *The Puffin.* Calton, T. & A.D. Poyser.

Harris, M.P. 1991. Breeding changes in British Common Murres and Atlantic Puffins, 1968–88. In: *Studies of high latitude seabirds. 2. Conservation biology of Thick-billed Murres in the Northwest Atlantic Ocean*, ed. by A.J. Gaston & R.D. Elliot. Occasional Paper 69, Ottawa, Canadian Wildlife Service. pp. 52–58.

Harris, M.P. 1993. Guillemot *Uria aalge*. In: *The New Atlas of Breeding Birds in Britain and Ireland*, ed. by D.W. Gibbons, J.M. Reid & R.A. Chapman. London, T. & A.D. Poyser. pp. 224–225.

Harris, M.P. 1993. Puffin *Fratercula arctica*. In: *The New Atlas of Breeding Birds in Britain and Ireland*, ed. by D.W. Gibbons, J.M. Reid & R.A. Chapman. London, T. & A.D. Poyser. pp. 230–231.

Harris, M.P. 1993. Razorbill *Alca torda*. In: *The New Atlas of Breeding Birds in Britain and Ireland*, ed. by D.W. Gibbons, J.M. Reid & R.A. Chapman. London, T. & A.D. Poyser. pp. 226–227.

Harris, M.P. 1997. Guillemot *Uria aalge*. In: *The EBCC Atlas of European Breeding Birds, Their Distribution and Abundance*, ed. by W.J.M. Hagemeijer & M.J. Blair. London, T. & A.D. Poyser. pp. 368–369.

Harris, M.P. 1997. Puffin *Fratercula arctica*. In: *The EBCC Atlas of European Breeding Birds, Their Distribution and Abundance*, ed. by W.J.M. Hagemeijer & M.J. Blair. London, T. & A.D. Poyser. pp. 376–377.

Harris, M.P. & Wanless, S. 1988. The breeding biology of Guillemots *Uria aalge* on the Isle of May over a six year period. *Ibis* 130: 172–192.

Harris, M.P. & Wanless, S. 1991. Population studies and conservation of Puffins *Fratercula arctica*. In: *Bird population studies: Relevance to conservation and management*, ed. by C.M. Perrins, J.-D. Lebreton & G.J.M. Hirons. Oxford, Oxford University Press. pp. 230–248.

Harris, M.P., Wanless, S. & Barton, T.R. 1996. Site use and fidelity in the Common Guillemot *Uria aalge*. *Ibis* 138: 399–404.

Harris, M.P., Wanless, S. & Smith, R.W.J. 1987. The breeding seabirds of the Firth of Forth, Scotland. *Proceedings of the Royal Society of Edinburgh* 93B: 521–533.

Harrison, J.A., Allan, D.G., Underhill, L.G., Herremans, M., Tree, A.J., Parker, V. & Brown, C.J. eds. 1997. *The Atlas of Southern African Birds*. Volume 1. Johannesburg, BirdLife South Africa.

Harvey, P. 1983. Breeding seabird populations, Isles of Scilly. *Nature Conservancy Council Report* ,SW England Region, Taunton.

Harvie-Brown, J.A. & Buckley, T.E. 1887. *A Vertebrate Fauna of Sutherland, Caithness and West Cromarty*. Edinburgh, David Douglas.

Harvie-Brown, J.A. & Buckley, T.E. 1888. *A Vertebrate Fauna of the Outer Hebrides*. Edinburgh, David Douglas.

Harvie-Brown, J.A. & Buckley, T.E. 1892. *A Vertebrate Fauna of Argyll and the Inner Hebrides*. David Douglas, Edinburgh.

Hearn, R.D. 1988. *The 1997 national census of Pink-footed Geese and Icelandic Greylag Geese in Britain*. Report to JNCC. Slimbridge, WWT. 14 pp.

Heath, M.F. & Evans, M.I. eds. 2000. *Important Bird Areas in Europe: priority sites for conservation*. 2 vols. Cambridge, BirdLife International (BirdLife Conservation Series No. 8).

Helle, P. 1986. Bird community dynamics in a boreal forest reserve: the importance of large-scale regional trends. *Annales Zoologici Fennici* 23: 157–166.

Henderson, I.G., Peach, W.J. & Baillie, S.R. 1993. *The hunting of Snipe and Woodcock in Europe: A ringing recovery analysis*. Thetford, BTO. (BTO Research Report No. 115)

Henriksen, K. 1991. Status och Bestandsutwikling hos Stor Regnspove *Numenius arquata* I Nordeuropa. *Danske Vildtundersögelser* 46. Miljøministeriet, Danmarks Miljøundersøgelser, Copenhagen.

Heredia, B., Rose, L. & Painter, M. 1996. *Globally threatened birds in Europe. Action plans*. Strasbourg, Council of Europe Publishing. 408 pp.

Heubeck, M., Mellor, R.M., Harvey, P.V., Mainwood, A.R. & Riddington, R. 1999. Estimating the population size and rate of decline of Kittiwakes *Rissa tridactyla* breeding in Shetland, 1981–97. *Bird Study* 46: 48–61.

Hildén, O. & Tasker, M. 1997. Razorbill *Alca torda*. In: *The EBCC Atlas of European Breeding Birds, Their Distribution and Abundance*, ed. by W.J.M. Hagemeijer & M.J. Blair. London, T. & A.D. Poyser. pp. 372–373.

Hill, D. 1988. Population dynamics of the Avocet *Recurvirostra avosetta* breeding in Britain. *Journal of Animal Ecology* 57: 638–669.

Hodge, T.N. ed. 1997. *Kent Bird Report 1995*. Kent, Kent Ornithological Society.

Hodges, J. 1994. *A Chough Conservation Strategy for Pembrokeshire*. Pembrokeshire, Pembrokeshire Coast National Park.

Holloway, S. 1996. *The Historical Atlas of Breeding Birds in Britain and Ireland, 1875–1900*. London, T. & A.D. Poyser.

Holmes, J.S. & Clement, P. 1996. *Fish-eating birds: proceedings of a seminar to review status, interactions with fisheries and licensing issues*. Peterborough, JNCC. (*UK Nature Conservation*, No. 15)

Holmes, J.S., Walker, D., Davies, P. & Carter, I. 2000. *The illegal persecution of raptors in England*. Peterborough, English Nature. (Research Report No. 343, 34 pp)

Holz, R. 1987. Populationsentwicklung des Sanregenpfeifers (*Charadrius hiaticula*) im sudwestlichen Ostseeraum: Uraschen und Konsequenzen veranderter Habitatnutzung. *Natur un Naturschutz in Mecklenburg* 25: 1–80.

Hope Jones, P. 1979. Roosting behaviour of Long-tailed Ducks in relation to possible oil pollution. *Wildfowl* 30: 155–158.

Horsfall, J.A. 1986. Coot *Fulica atra*. In: *The Atlas of Wintering Birds in Britain and Ireland*, ed. by P. Lack. Calton, T. & A.D. Poyser. pp. 176–177.

Hötker, H. 1991. Waders breeding on wet grasslands in the Countries of the European Community —a brief summary of current knowledge of population sizes and population trends. In: Hötker, H. (ed.), Waders breeding on wet grasslands. *Wader Study Group Bulletin* No. 61 *Supplement* April 1991. pp. 50–55.

Hoyo, J. del, Elliott, A. & Sargatal, J. eds. 1992. *Handbook of the Birds of the World. Volume 1: Ostrich to Ducks*. Barcelona, Lynx Edicions. 696 pp.

Hoyo, J. del, Elliott, A. & Sargatal, J. eds. 1994. *Handbook of the Birds of the World. Volume 2: New World Vultures to Guineafowl*. Barcelona, Lynx Edicions. 638 pp.

Hoyo, J. del, Elliot A. & Sargatal, J. eds. 1996. *Handbook of the Birds of the World. Volume 3: Hoatzin to Auks*. Barcelona, Lynx Edicions. 821 pp.

Hudson, A.V. & Furness, R.W. 1988. *Utilisation of discarded fish by scavenging seabirds behind whitefish trawlers in Shetland*. Journal of Zoology, London 215: 151–166.

Hudson, A.V., Stowe, T. & Aspinall, S.J. 1990. Status and distribution of Corncrakes in Britain in 1988. *British Birds* 83: 173–187.

Hudson, R., Tucker, G.M. & Fuller, R.J. 1994. Lapwing *Vanellus vanellus* populations in relation to agricultural changes: a review. In: *The ecology and conservation of Lapwings* Vanellus vanellus, ed. by G.M. Tucker, S.M. Davies & R.J. Fuller. Peterborough, JNCC. (*UK Nature Conservation*, No. 9, pp. 1–33)

Hughes, S.W.M., Bacon, P. & Flegg, J.J.M. 1979. The 1975 census of the Great Crested Grebe in Britain. *Bird Study* 26: 213–226.

Hulscher, J.B. 1997. Oystercatcher *Haematopus ostralegus*. In: *The EBCC Atlas of European Breeding Birds: Their Distribution and Abundance*, ed. by W.J.M. Hagemeijer & M.J. Blair. London, T. & A.D. Poyser. pp. 246–247.

Hutchinson, C.D. 1989. *Birds in Ireland.* Calton, T. & A.D. Poyser.

Imboden, C. 1974. Zug, Fremdansiedlung und Brutperiods des Kiebitz *Vanellus vanellus* in Europa. *Ornithologische Beobachter* 71: 5–134.

Insley, H. & Young, L. 1981. Autumn passage of Ringed Plovers through Southampton Water. *Ringing & Migration* 3: 157–164.

Jackson, D.B. 1994. Breeding dispersal and site-fidelity in three monogamous wader species in the Western Isles, U.K. *Ibis* 136: 463–473.

Jackson, D.B. & Green, R.E. 2000. The importance of the introduced hedgehog (*Erinaceus europaeus*) as a predator of the eggs of waders (Charadii) on machair in South Uist, Scotland. *Biological Conservation* 93: 333–348.

James, P. ed. 1996. *Birds of Sussex.* Sussex, Sussex Ornithological Society.

Janzen, D.H. 1983. No park is an island, increase in interference from outside as park size decreases. *Oikos* 41: 402–410.

Jenkins, D.J. (*ed*) 1991. Proceedings of the 5th International Symposium on Grouse. *Ornis Scandinavica* 22: 176–302.

JNCC 1999. *The Birds Directive. Selection guidelines for Special Protection Areas.* Peterborough, JNCC. 6 pp.

Joensen, A.H. 1976. Moulting and wintering seaducks in Denmark. In: *Bird Migration.* Valgus, Tallinn.

Johnston, J.L. 1999. A Naturalist's Shetland. London, T. & A.D. Poyser.

Jones, P.H. 1979. Roosting behaviour of Long-tailed Ducks in relation to possible oil pollution. *Wildfowl* 30: 155–158

Jönsson, P.E. 1988. *The ecology of the southern Dunlin* Calidris alpina schinzii. PhD Thesis, University of Lund, Sweden.

Jönsson, P.E. 1991. Reproduction and survival in a declining population of the Southern Dunlin *Calidris alpina schinzii*. In: Waders Breeding on Wet Grassland, ed. by H. Hötker. *Wader Study Group Bulletin* 61 *Supplement*: 56–68.

Kear, J. 1963. The history of potato-eating by wildfowl in Britain. *Wildfowl Trust Annual Report* 14: 54–65.

Keller, V. & Hario, M. 1997 Eider *Somateria mollissima*. In: *The EBCC Atlas of European Breeding Birds: Their Distribution and Abundance*, ed. by W.J.M. Hagemeijer & M.J. Blair. London, T. & A.D. Poyser. pp. 110–111.

Kennedy, P.G., Ruttledge, R.F. & Scroope, C.S. 1954. *Birds of Ireland.* Edinburgh, Oliver & Boyd.

Kershaw, M. 1998a. Long-term population trends in wintering Pintail (*Anas acuta*) in Great Britain 1966–95. Slimbridge, WWT unpublished report to JNCC.

Kershaw, M. 1998b. Trends in the number of wintering Pochard (*Aythya ferina* L.) in Britain, 1966–1993, at a regional, habitat and site level. Slimbridge, WWT report to WeBS partners.

Kershaw, M. & Hughes, B. 1997. Trends in the numbers of Cormorants *Phalacrocorax carbo*, Goosanders *Mergus merganser* and Red-breasted Merganser *Mergus serrator* wintering in the UK. Slimbridge. WWT report to BTO.

Kirby, J.S. 1995a. Winter population estimates for selected waterfowl species in Britain. *Biological Conservation* 73: 189–198.

Kirby, J.S. 1995b. *Distribution and dynamics of wintering waders in Britain with particular reference to weather.* PhD thesis, Open University. 293 pp.

Kirby, J.S. & Lack, P. 1993. Spatial dynamics of wintering Lapwings and Golden Plovers in Britain and Ireland, 1981–82 to 1983–84. *Bird Study* 40: 38–50.

Kirby, J.S. & Mitchell, C. 1993. Distribution and status of wintering Shoveler in Great Britain. *Bird Study* 40: 170–180.

Kirby, J.S., Clee, C. & Seager, V. 1993. Impact and extent of recreational disturbance to wader roosts on the Dee estuary: some preliminary results. *Wader Study Group Bulletin* 68: 53–58.

Kirby, J.S., Evans, R.J. & Fox, A.D. 1993. Wintering seaducks in Britain and Ireland: populations, threats, conservation and research priorities. *Aquatic Conservation: Marine and Freshwater Ecosystems* 3: 105–117.

Kirby, J.S., Gilburn, A.S. & Sellers, R.M. 1995. Status, distribution and habitat use by Cormorants *Phalacrocorax carbo* wintering in Britain. *Ardea* 83: 93–102.

Kirby, J.S., Rees, E.C., Merne, O.J. & Garðarsson, A. 1992. International census of Whooper Swans *Cygnus cygnus* in Britain, Ireland and Iceland: January 1991. *Wildfowl* 43: 20–26.

Kirby, J.S., Salmon, D.G., Atkinson-Willes, G.L. & Cranswick, P.A. 1995. Index numbers for waterbird populations. *Journal of Applied Ecology* 32: 536–551.

Kirby, J.S., West, R., Scott, D.A., Davidson, N.C., Piersma, T., Hötker, H. & Stroud, D.A. in prep. *Atlas of wader populations in Africa and Western Eurasia, Phase 1.* International Wader Study Group & Wetlands International.

Klemm, C de. & Shine, C. 1993. *Biological Diversity Conservation and the Law. Legal mechanisms for conserving species and ecosystems.* IUCN Environmental Policy and Law Paper No. 29. IUCN.

Kłosowscy, G., Kłosowscy, S. & Kłosowscy, T. 1991. *Ptaki biebrzańskich bagien.* [*The birds of Biebrza marshes*]. Warszawa, Poland. 294 pp.

Knox, A.G. 1990a. The identification of Crossbill and Scottish Crossbill. *British Birds* 83: 89–94.

Knox, A.G. 1990b. The systematic breeding of Common and Scottish Crossbills *Loxia curvirostra* and *L. scotica* and the evolution of crossbills. *Ibis* 132: 454–466.

Knox, A.G. & Bell, M.V. 1979. Systematic list. In: *North-East Scotland Bird Report 1978.* Aberdeen, North-East Scotland Bird Club. pp. 6–31.

Koskimies, P. 1993. *Population sizes and recent trends of breeding birds in the Nordic countries.* Helsinki, Vesi- Ja Ymparistohallitus. 47 pp.

Kramer, L. 1992. *Focus on European Environmental Law.* London, Sweet & Maxwell. 321 pp.

Lack, P. 1986. *The Atlas of Wintering Birds in Britain and Ireland.* Calton, T. & A.D. Poyser.

Lammi, E. 1997. Red-breasted Merganser *Mergus serrator.* In: *The EBCC Atlas of European Breeding Birds: Their Distribution and Abundance,* ed. by W.J.M. Hagemeijer & M.J. Blair. London, T. & A.D. Poyser. pp. 124–125.

Lappo, E.G. 1998. Mapping breeding range structure of tundra waders in Russia. In: Migration and international conservation of waders. Research and conservation on North Asian, African and European flyways, by H. Hötker, E. Lebedeva, P.S. Tomkovich, J. Gromadzka, N.C. Davidson, J. Evans, D.A. Stroud & R.B. West. *International Wader Studies* 10: 145–151.

Lappo, E.G. & Tomkovich, P.S. 1998. Breeding distribution of Dunlin *Calidris alpina* in Russia. In: Migration and international conservation of waders. Research and conservation on North Asian, African and European flyways, by H. Hötker, E. Lebedeva, P.S. Tomkovich, J. Gromadzka, N.C. Davidson, J. Evans, D.A. Stroud & R.B. West. *International Wader Studies* 10: 152–169.

Laubek, B. 1998. *The Northwest European Whooper Swan (*Cygnus cygnus*) population: ecological and management aspects of an expanding waterfowl population.* PhD Thesis, University of Aarhus, Denmark.

Laubek, B., Nilsson, L., Wieloch, M., Koffijberg, K., Sudfelt, C. & Follestad, A. 1999. Distribution, numbers and habitat choice of the NW European Whooper Swan *Cygnus cygnus* population: results of an international census in January 1995. *Vogelwelt* 120: 141–154.

Lawton Roberts, J. & Bowman, N. 1986. Diet and ecology of Short-eared Owls *Asio flammeus* breeding on heather moor. *Bird Study* 33: 12–17.

Lebedeva, E.A. 1998. Waders in agricultural habitats of European Russia. In: Migration and international conservation of waders. Research and conservation on North Asian, African and European flyways, by H. Hötker, E. Lebedeva, P.S. Tomkovich, J. Gromadzka, N.C. Davidson, J Evans, D.A. Stroud & R.B. West. *International Wader Studies* 10: 315–324.

Leibak, E., Lilleleht, V. & Veromann, H. eds. 1994. *Birds in Estonia: status, distribution and numbers.* Tallinn, Estonian Academy Publishers.

Lindell, L., Mellin, M., Musil, P., Przybysz, J. & Zimmerman, H. 1995. Status and population development of breeding Cormorants *Phalacrocorax carbo sinensis* of the central European flyway. *Ardea* 83: 81–92.

Lindsay, R.A., Charman, D.J., Everingham, F., O'Reilly, R.M., Palmer, M.A., Rowell, T.A. & Stroud, D.A. 1988. *The Flow Country: the peatlands of Caithness and Sutherland.* Peterborough, Nature Conservancy Council. 174 pp.

Little, B. & Furness, R.W. 1985. Long-distance moult migration by British Goosanders *Mergus merganser. Ringing & Migration* 6: 77–82.

Lloyd, C., Tasker, M.L. & Partridge, K. 1991. *The status of seabirds in Britain and Ireland.* London, T. & A.D. Poyser. 355 pp.

Lock, L. & Cook, K. 1998. The Little Egret in Britain: a successful colonist. *British Birds* 91: 273–280.

Love, J.A. 1983. *The return of the Sea Eagle.* Cambridge, Cambridge University Press.

Lovegrove, R., Williams, G. & Williams, I. 1994. *Birds in Wales.* London, T. & A.D. Poyser.

Low, Rev. G. 1879. *A Tour through the islands of Orkney and Shetland containing hints relative their Ancient, Modern and Natural History collected in 1774.* Kirkwall, Orkney. 223 pp.

Lowe, G. ed. 1998. *Suffolk Birds*, Volume 47. Ipswich, Suffolk Naturalists' Society.

Lyngs, P. 1992. Ynglefuglene på Graesholmen 1925–90. *Dansk Ornitologisk Forenings Tidsskrift* 86: 1–93.

MacMillan, A.T. 1969. Scottish Bird Report 1968. *Scottish Birds* 5: 317.

Madders, M., Leckie, F.M., Watson, J. & McKay, C.R. 1998. Distribution and foraging habitat preferences of Choughs on the Oa peninsula, Islay. *Scottish Birds* 19: 280–289.

Madge, S. & Burn, H. 1988. *Wildfowl: an Identification Guide to the Ducks, Geese and Swans of the World.* Bromley, Helm.

Madsen, J. 1991. Status and trends of goose populations in the Western Palearctic in the 1980s. *Ardea* 79: 113–121.

Madsen, J., Bregnballe, T. & Hastrup, A. 1992. Impact of the Arctic Fox *Alopex lagopus* on nesting success of geese in south-east Svalbard, 1989. *Polar Research* 11: 35–39.

Madsen, J., Bregnballe, T. & Mehlum, F. 1989. Study of the breeding ecology and behaviour of the Svalbard population of Light-bellied Brent Goose *Branta bernicla hrota. Polar Research* 7: 1–21.

Madsen, J., Cracknell, G. & Fox, A.D. (eds.) 1999. *Goose populations of the Western Palearctic: a review of status and distribution.* Wetlands International Publication No. 48/NERI, Denmark. 343 pp.

Madsen, J., Reed, A. & Andreev, A. 1996. Status and trends of geese (*Anser* sp., *Branta* sp.) in the world: a review, updating and evaluation. In: *Proceedings of Anatidae 2000*, ed. by M. Birkan, J. van Vessem, P. Havet, J. Madsen, B. Trolliet & M. Moser. *Gibier Faune Sauvage, Game Wildlife* 13.

Madsen, J., Kuijken, E., Meire, P., Cottaar, F., Haitjema, T., Nicolaisen, P.I., Bønes, T. & Mehlum, F. 1999. Pink-footed Goose *Anser brachyrhynchus*: Svalbard. In: *Goose populations of the Western Palearctic: a review of status and distribution*, by J. Madsen, G. Cracknell & A.D. Fox. Denmark, Wetlands International Publication No. 48/NERI. pp. 82–93.

Mainwood, A.R. 1996. *The post-moult movements and winter distribution of native Greylag Geese* (Anser anser) *in Sutherland and Caithness*. SNH report.

Marquiss, M., Ratcliffe, D.A. & Roxburgh, L.R. 1985. The numbers, breeding success and diet of Golden Eagles in Southern Scotland in relation to changes in land use. *Biological Conservation* 34: 121–140.

Martin, A.P. & Baird, D. 1988. Lemming cycles – which Palearctic migrants are affected? *Bird Study* 35: 143–145.

Marchant, J.H., Hudson, R., Carter, S. & Whittington, P. 1990. *Population trends in British breeding birds.* Tring, BTO/NCC. 300 pp.

Mason, C.F. & MacDonald, S.M. 1999. Habitat use by Lapwings and Golden Plovers in a largely arable landscape. *Bird Study* 46: 89–99.

Mathers, R.G. 1995. *The distribution and abundance of Pale-bellied Brent Geese and Wigeon on Strangford Lough; the roles of competition, food availability and human activity.* Unpublished PhD thesis, Queen's University of Belfast.

Mathew, M.A. 1894. *The birds of Pembrokeshire and its islands*. London, Porter. 131 pp.

Mayabayashi, Y. & Mundkur, T. 1999. *Atlas of key sites for Anatidae in the East Asian Flyway.* Wetlands International-Asia Pacific. 148 pp.

Mayhew, P.W. 1988. The daily energy intake of European Wigeon in winter. *Ornis Scandinavica* 19: 217–233.

Mayr, E. 1970. *Populations, species and evolution.* Cambridge, Massachusetts, USA, Harvard University Press.

McElwaine, J.G., Wells, J.H. & Bowler, J.M. 1995. Preliminary results from a study of the winter movements of Whooper Swans visiting Ireland. *Irish Birds* 5: 265–278.

McGhie, H.A. 1994. Discovery of the first British clutch of Slavonian Grebe eggs in a museum collection. *Scottish Birds* 17: 166–167.

McGrady, M.J., McLeod, D.R., Petty, S.J., Grant, J.R. & Bainbridge, I.P. 1997. *Golden Eagles and forestry.* Roslin, Forestry Commission Research Information Note.

Mead, C. 1989. Mono-kill and Auk netfax. *British Trust for Ornithology News 163*: 1 & 8.

Mednis, A. & Zomerdijk, P. 1997. Tufted Duck *Aythya fuligula*. In: *The EBCC Atlas of European Breeding Birds: Their Distribution and Abundance*, ed. by W.J.M. Hagemeijer & M.J. Blair. London, T. & A.D. Poyser. pp. 106–107.

Meek, E.R., Booth, C.J., Reynolds, P. & Ribbands, B. 1985. Breeding Skuas in Orkney. *Seabird* 8: 21–33.

Meek, E.R., Rebecca, G.W., Ribbands, B & Fairclough, K. 1998. Orkney Hen Harriers: a major population decline in the absence of persecution. *Scottish Birds* 19: 290–298.

Meininger, P.L. & de Kraker, K. 1992. De Middelste Zaagbek *Mergus serrator* als broedvogel in het Deltagebied, ZW-Nederland, 1977–91. *Limosa* 65: 49–51.

Meininger, P.L., Blomert, A.-M. & Marteijn, E.C.L. 1991. Watervogelsterfte in het Deltagebied, ZW-Nederland, gedurende de drie koude winters van 1985, 1986 en 1987. [Mortality of waterbirds in the Delta area, S.W. Netherlands during the three cold winters of 1985, 1986 and 1987.] *Limosa* 64: 89–102.

Meininger, P.L., Schekkerman, H. & van Roomen, M.W.J. 1995. Populatieschattingen en 1%-normen van in Nederland voorkomende watervogelsoorten: voorstellen voor standaardisatie. [Population estimates and 1%-levels for waterbird species occurring in The Netherlands: suggestions for standardisation.] *Limosa* 68: 41–48.

Meltofte, H., Blew, J., Frikke, J., Rösner, H.-U. & Smit, C.J. 1994. Numbers and distribution of waterbirds in the Wadden Sea. Results and evaluation of 36 simultaneous counts in the Dutch-German-Danish Wadden Sea 1980–1991. *IWRB Publication* 34/*Wader Study Group Bulletin* 74, Special issue.

Merne, O.J. 1972. Bewick's Swans feeding on waste potatoes and other agricultural crops. *British Birds* 65: 394–395.

Merne, O.J. & Walsh, A. 1994. Barnacle Geese in Ireland, spring 1993 and 1994. *Irish Birds* 5: 151–156.

Merne, O.J., Boertmann, D., Boyd, H., Mitchell, C., Ó Briain, M., Reed, A. & Sigfusson, A. 1999. Light-bellied Brent Goose *Branta bernicla hrota*: Canada. In: *Goose populations of the Western Palearctic: a review of status and distribution*, by J. Madsen, G. Cracknell & A.D. Fox. Denmark, Wetlands International Publication No. 48/NERI. pp. 298–311.

Mikkola, H. 1983. *Owls of Europe.* Calton, T. & A.D. Poyser.

Mikola, J., Miettinen, M., Lehikoinen, E. & Lehtilä, K. 1994. The effects of disturbance caused by boating on survival and behaviour of Velvet Scoter *Melanitta fusca* ducklings. *Biological Conservation* 67: 119–124.

Milne, P. & O'Sullivan, O. 1999. Forty-fifth Irish Bird Report. *Irish Birds* 6: 285–312.

Mitchell, C. 1994. *The movement of British ringed Shoveler.* Unpublished report, WWT, Slimbridge.

Mitchell, C. in press. Wigeon *Anas penelope*. In: *The Migration Atlas: Movements of the Birds of Britain and Ireland*, by C.V. Wernham, M.P. Toms, J.H. Marchant, J.A. Clark, G.M. Siriwardena & S.R. Baillie. London, T. & A.D. Poyser.

Mitchell, C. & Sigfusson, A. 1999. Greylag Goose *Anser anser*: Iceland. In: *Goose populations of the Western Palearctic: a review of status and distribution*, by J. Madsen, G. Cracknell & A.D. Fox. Denmark, Wetlands International Publication No. 48/NERI. pp. 162–171.

Mitchell, C., MacDonald, R. & Boyer P. 1995. *Greylag Geese on the Uists.* Slimbridge, WWT report to JNCC.

Mitchell, C., Fox, A.D., Boyd, H., Sigfusson, A. & Boertmann, D. 1999. Pink-footed Goose *Anser brachyrhynchus*: Iceland/Greenland. In: *Goose populations of the Western Palearctic: a review of status and distribution*, by J. Madsen, G. Cracknell & A.D. Fox. Denmark, Wetlands International Publication No. 48/NERI. pp. 68–81.

Monaghan, P. 1988. The background to chough studies in Britain. In: *Choughs and Land-use in Europe. Proceedings of an International Workshop on the Conservation of the Chough, Pyrrhocorax pyrrhocorax, in the EC. 11–14 November 1988*, ed. by E.M. Bignal & D.J. Curtis. Argyll, Scottish Chough Study Group. pp. 4–8.

Monaghan, P. 1992. Seabirds and sandeels: the conflict between exploitation and conservation in the northern North Sea. *Biodiversity and Conservation* 1: 98–111.

Monaghan, P. & Coulson, J.C. 1977. The status of large gulls nesting on buildings. *Bird Study* 24: 89–104.

Monaghan, P., Uttley, J.D. & Burns, M.D. 1992. Effect of changes in food availability on reproductive effort in Arctic Terns *Sterna paradisaea*. *Ardea* 80: 71–81.

Monaghan, P., Uttley, J.D., Burns, M.D., Thaine, C. & Blackwood, J. 1989. The relationship between food supply, reproductive effort and breeding success in Arctic Terns *Sterna paradisaea*. *Journal of Animal Ecology* 38: 261–274.

Monval, J.-Y. & Pirot, J.-Y. 1989. *Results of the IWRB International Waterfowl Census 1967–1986.* Slimbridge, IWRB. (IWRB Special Publication No. 8)

Mooij, J.H., Faragó, S. & Kirby, J.S. 1999. White-fronted Goose *Anser albifrons albifrons*. In: *Goose populations of the Western Palearctic: a review of status and distribution*, by J. Madsen, G. Cracknell & A.D. Fox. Denmark, Wetlands International Publication No. 48/NERI. pp. 94–128.

Moore, N.W. & Walker, C.H. 1964. Organo-chloride insecticide resides in wild birds. *Nature* 201: 1072–1073.

Morozov, V.V. 1998. Distribution of breeding waders in the north-east European Russian tundras. In: *Migration and international conservation of waders. Research and conservation on North Asian, African and European flyways*, by H. Hötker, E. Lebedeva, P.S. Tomkovich, J. Gromadzka, N.C. Davidson, J. Evans, D.A. Stroud & R.B. West. *International Wader Studies* 10: 186–194.

Morris, A., Burgess, D., Fuller, R.J., Evans, A.D. & Smith, K.W. 1994. The status and distribution of Nightjars *Caprimulgus europaeus* in Britain in 1992. *Bird Study* 41: 181–191.

Moser, M. 1987. Importance of UK estuaries for waders and wildfowl. *RSPB Conservation Review* 1: 34–36.

Moser, M. 1988. Limits to the numbers of Grey Plovers *Pluvialis squatarola* wintering on British estuaries: an analysis of long-term population trends. *Journal of Applied Ecology* 25: 473–485.

Moser, M. & Carrier, M. 1983. Patterns of population turnover in Ringed Plovers and Turnstones during their spring passage through the Solway Firth in 1983. *Wader Study Group Bulletin* 39: 37–41.

Moser, M. & Summers, R.W. 1987. Wader populations on the non-estuarine coasts of Britain and Northern Ireland: results of the 1984–85 Winter Shorebird Count. *Bird Study* 34: 71–81.

Moser, M., Ferns, P. & Baillie, S. 1985. BTO/WSG West Coast Spring Passage Project. *Wader Study Group Bulletin* 43: 9–13

Moser, M.E., Broad, R.A., Dennis, R.H. & Madders, M. 1986. The distribution and abundance of some coastal birds on the west and north-west coasts of Scotland in winter. *Scottish Birds* 14: 61–67.

Moss, R. 1994. Decline of capercaillie (*Tetrao urogallus*) in Scotland. *Gibier Faune Sauvage* 11 (special number): 217–222.

Moss, R. & Picozzi, N. 1994. *Management of forests for capercaillie in Scotland*. London, HMSO. (Forestry Commission Bulletin No. 113)

Moss, R., Picozzi, N., Summers, R.W. & Baines, D. 2000. Capercaillie *Tetrao urogallus* in Scotland – demography of a declining population. *Ibis* 142: 259–267.

Mudge, G.P. & Allen, D.S. 1980. Wintering seaducks in the Moray and Dornoch Firths. *Wildfowl* 31: 123–172.

Mudge, G.P., Dennis, R.H., Talbot, T.R. & Broad, R.A. 1991. Changes in the breeding status of Black-throated Divers in Scotland. *Scottish Birds* 16: 77–84.

Mullie, W.C. & Porter, E.P.R. 1977. Aantallen verspreiding et terreinkeus van die Kleine Zwaan bij vijf landelijke tellingen in 1976 en 1977. *Watervogels* 2: 85–96.

Murray, S. & Wanless, S. 1986. The status of the Gannet in Scotland in 1984–85. *Scottish Birds* 14: 74–85.

Murray, S. & Wanless, S. 1997. The status of the Gannet in Scotland in 1994–95. *Scottish Birds* 19: 10–27.

Myers, J.P. 1984. Spacing behavior of non-breeding shorebirds. In: *Behavior of marine animals, Vol. 6: shorebirds: migration and foraging behavior*, ed. by J. Burger & B.L. Olla. New York, Plenum Press. pp. 271–322.

Myers, J.P., Schick, C.T. & Castro, G. 1986. Structure in Sanderling populations: the magnitude of intra- and inter-year dispersal during the non-breeding season. In: *Acta XIX Congressus Internationalis Ornithologica*, ed. by H. Ouellet. Ottawa, University of Ottawa Press. pp. 604–615.

Nature Conservancy Council 1983. *Ramsar sites and Special Protection Areas*. London, Nature Conservancy Council. 13 pp.

Nature Conservancy Council 1985. *Nature conservation importance of Duich Moss, Scotland, United Kingdom*. Report to European Commission. Peterborough, Nature Conservancy Council.

Nature Conservancy Council 1989. *Guidelines for selection of biological SSSIs*. Peterborough, Nature Conservancy Council. 288 pp.

Nelson, J.R. 1978. *The Sulidae. Gannets and Boobies*. Oxford University Press. 1,012 pp.

Nethersole-Thompson, D. 1951. *The Greenshank*. London, Collins.

Nethersole-Thompson, D. & Nethersole-Thompson, M. 1979. *Greenshanks*. Calton, T. & A.D. Poyser.

Nethersole-Thompson, D. & Nethersole-Thompson, M. 1986. *Waders: their breeding haunts and watchers*. London, T. & A.D. Poyser.

Nettleship, D.N. & Evans, P.G.H. 1985. Distribution and status of the Atlantic Alcidae. In: *The Atlantic Alcidae*, ed. by D.N. Nettleship & T.R. Birkhead. London, Academic Press. pp. 53–154.

Nevo, A.J. del, Dunn, E.K., Medeiros, F.M., Le Grand, G., Akers, P., Avery, M.I. & Monteiro, L. 1993. The status of Roseate Terns *Sterna dougallii* and Common Terns *Sterna hirundo* in the Azores. *Seabird* 15: 30–37.

Newbery, P. 1998. *Species Action Plan 1559 Chough* Pyrrhocorax pyrrhocorax. Sandy, RSPB.

Newton, I. 1994. Current population levels of diurnal raptors in Britain. *The Raptor* 21: 17–21.

Newton, I. & Haas, M.B. 1988. Pollutants in Merlin eggs and their effects on breeding. *British Birds* 81: 258–269.

Newton, I., Bogan, E., Meek, E.R. & Little, B. 1982. Organochlorine compounds and shell thinning in British Merlins *Falco columbarius*. *Ibis* 124: 328–335.

Newton, S.F. & Percival, S.M. 1989. Barnacle Geese on Coll and Tiree. In: *Birds on Coll and Tiree: status, habitats and conservation*, ed. by D.A. Stroud. Edinburgh, Nature Conservancy Council/Scottish Ornithologists' Club. pp. 115–128.

Nicoll, M., Summers, R.W., Underhill, L.G., Brockie, K. & Rae, R. 1988. Regional, seasonal and annual variations in the structure of Purple Sandpiper *Calidris maritima* populations in Britain. *Ibis* 130: 221–233.

Nikiforov, M.E. & Mongin, E.A. 1998. Breeding waders of Belarus: number estimates and recent population trends. In: Tomkovich, P.S. & Lebedeva, E.A. eds. *Breeding Waders in Eastern Europe – 2000*. Volume 1. Russian Bird Conservation Union, Moscow. pp. 93–96.

Nikolaev, V.I. 1998. The importance of the peatlands of the Upper Volga area as habitats for breeding waders. In: Migration and international conservation of waders. Research and conservation on North Asian, African and European flyways, by H. Hötker, E. Lebedeva, P.S. Tomkovich, J. Gromadzka, N.C. Davidson, J. Evans, D.A. Stroud & R.B. West. *International Wader Studies* 10: 291–298.

Nilsson, L., van den Bergh, L. & Madsen, J. 1999. Taiga Bean Goose *Anser fabalis fabalis*. In: *Goose populations of the Western Palearctic: a review of status and distribution*, by J. Madsen, G. Cracknell & A.D. Fox. Denmark, Wetlands International Publication No. 48/NERI. pp. 20–36.

Nisbet, I.C.T. 1959. Bewick's Swans in the British Isles in the winters 1954–55 and 1955–56. *British Birds* 48: 533–537.

Noble, D., Bashford, R.I., Marchant, J.H., Baillie, S.R. & Gregory, R.D. 1999. *The Breeding Bird Survey 1998*. Thetford: BTO, JNCC, & RSPB. 16 pp.

Norris, C.A. 1945. Summary of a report on the distribution and status of the Corncrake (*Crex crex*). *British Birds* 38: 142–168.

Norris, C.A. 1947. Report on the distribution and status of the Corncrake. *British Birds* 40: 226–244.

Norris, C.A. 1953. The birds of Bardsey Island in 1952. *British Birds* 46: 131–137.

Norris, K., Bannister, R.C.A. & Walker, P.W. 1998. Changes in the number of oystercatchers *Haematopus ostralegus* wintering in the Burry Inlet in relation to the biomass of cockles *Cerastoderma edule* and its commercial exploitation. *Journal of Applied Ecology* 35: 75–85.

Norris, K. & Buisson, R. 1994. Sea-level rise and its impact upon coastal birds in the UK. *RSPB Conservation Review* 8: 63–71.

Norriss, D.W. & Wilson, H.J. 1993. Seasonal and long-term changes in habitat selection by Greenland White-fronted Geese *Anser albifrons flavirostris* in Ireland. *Wildfowl* 44: 7–18.

Nugteren, J. van 1994. *Brent Geese in the Wadden Sea. Proceedings of the international workshop 'Brent Geese in the Wadden Sea', Leeuwarden, The Netherlands, 22–23 September 1994*. The Netherlands, LVBW. 216 pp.

Nugteren, J. van 1997. *Dark-bellied Brent Goose* Branta bernicla bernicla *Flyway Management Plan*. Information and Reference Centre for Nature Management/Dutch Society of the Preservation of the Wadden Sea. Wageningen. 198 pp.

OAG Münster 1998. Mass of Ruffs *Philomachus pugnax* wintering in west Africa. In: *Migration and international conservation of waders. Research and conservation on North Asian, African and European flyways*, by H. Hötker, E. Lebedeva, P.S. Tomkovich, J. Gromadzka, N.C. Davidson, J. Evans, D.A. Stroud & R.B. West. *International Wader Studies* 10: 435–440.

Ó Briain, M. & Healy, B. 1991. Winter distribution of Light-bellied Brent Geese *Branta bernicla hrota* in Ireland. *Ardea* 79: 317–326.

O'Brien, M. & Smith, K.W. 1992. Changes in the status of waders breeding on wet lowland grasslands in England and Wales between 1982 and 1989. *Bird Study* 39: 165–176.

O'Brien, M., Newbery, P. & Suddaby, D. 1997. Action for breeding Red-necked Phalaropes in Scotland. *RSPB Conservation Review* 11: 74–79.

O'Donnel, C. & Fjeldså, J. 1997. (compilers) *Grebes –ß Status Survey and Conservation Action Plan*. IUCN/SSC Grebe Specialist Group. Gland, IUCN.

Ogilvie, M.A. & St Joseph, A.K.M. 1976. Dark-bellied Brent Geese in Britain and Europe, 1955–1976. *British Birds* 69: 422–439.

Ogilvie, M.A. & the Rare Breeding Birds Panel 1996. Rare breeding birds in the United Kingdom in 1993. *British Birds* 89: 61–91.

Ogilvie, M.A. & the Rare Breeding Birds Panel 1998. Rare breeding birds in the United Kingdom in 1995. *British Birds* 91: 417–447.

Ogilvie, M.A. & the Rare Breeding Birds Panel 1999a. Rare breeding birds in the United Kingdom in 1996. *British Birds* 92: 120–154.

Ogilvie, M.A. & the Rare Breeding Birds Panel 1999b. Non-native birds breeding in the United Kingdom in 1996. *British Birds* 92: 176–182.

Ogilvie, M.A., Boertmann, D., Cabot, D., Merne, O., Percival, S.M. & Sigfusson, A. 1999. Barnacle Goose *Branta leucopsis*: Greenland. In: *Goose populations of the Western Palearctic: a review of status and distribution*, by J. Madsen, G. Cracknell & A.D. Fox. Denmark, Wetlands International Publication No. 48/NERI. pp. 246–256.

Olney, P.J.S. 1963. The food and feeding habits of the Tufted Duck *Aythya fuligula*. *Ibis* 105: 55–62.

Olney, P.J.S. 1964. The food of Mallard collected from coastal and estuarine areas. *Proceedings of the Zoological Society, London* 140: 169–210.

Olney, P.J.S. 1965. The autumn and winter feeding biology of certain sympatric ducks. *Transactions of the VI Congregation of the International Union for Game Biology, Bournemouth*, 1963: 309–322.

Olney, P.J.S. 1968. The food and feeding habits of Pochard. *Biological Conservation* 1: 71–78.

O'Meara, M. 1979. Distribution and numbers of corncrakes in Ireland in 1978. *Irish Birds* 1: 381–405

O'Meara, M. 1986. Corncrake declines in seven areas, 1978–85. *Irish Birds* 3: 237–244.

Osieck, E.R. & Mörzer Bruyns, M.F. 1981. *Important bird areas in the European Community*. Cambridge, International Council for Bird Preservation. 194 pp.

Ovenden, G.N., Swash, A.R.H. & Smallshire, D. 1998. Agri-environment schemes and their contribution to the conservation of biodiversity in England. *Journal of Applied Ecology* 35: 955–960.

Owen, D.A.L. 1989. Factors affecting the status of the Chough in England and Wales; 1780–1980. In: *Choughs and Land-use in Europe. Proceedings of an International Workshop on the Conservation of the Chough*, Pyrrhocorax pyrrhocorax, *in the EC. 11–14 November 1988*, ed. by E.M. Bignal & D.J. Curtis. Kintyre, Scottish Chough Study Group. pp. 72–80.

Owen, M. 1975. An assessment of fecal analysis technique in waterfowl feeding studies. *Journal of Wildlife Management 39*: 271–279.

Owen, M. 1976. Factors affecting the distribution of geese in the British Isles. *Wildfowl* 27: 143–147.

Owen, M. & Cadbury, C.J. 1975. The ecology and mortality of swans at the Ouse Washes, England. *Wildfowl* 26: 31–42.

Owen, M. & Kear, J. 1972. Food and feeding habits. In: *The Swans*, ed. by P Scott & The Wildfowl Trust. London, Michael Joseph.

Owen, M. & Kerbes, R.H. 1971. On the autumn food of Barnacle Geese at Caerlaverock National Nature Reserve. *Wildfowl 22*: 114–119.

Owen, M. & Norderhaug, M. 1977. Population dynamics of Barnacle Geese *Branta leucopsis* breeding in Svalbard, 1948–1976. *Ornis Scandinavica* 8: 161–174.

Owen, M. & Campbell, C.R.G. 1974. Recent studies on Barnacle Geese at Caerlaverock. *Scottish Birds* 8: 180–193.

Owen, M. & Gullestad, N. 1984. Migration routes of Svalbard Barnacle Geese *Branta leucopsis* with a preliminary report on the importance of the Bjørnøya staging area. *Norsk Polarinstitut Skrifter* 181: 67–77.

Owen, M., Atkinson-Willes, G.L. & Salmon, D.G. 1986. *Wildfowl in Great Britain; second edition*. Cambridge, Cambridge University Press.

Owen, M., Black, J.M., Agger, M.C. & Campbell, C.R.G. 1987. The use of the Solway Firth by an increasing population of Barnacle Geese in relation to changes in refuge management. *Biological Conservation* 39: 63–81.

Pain, D., Amiard-Triquet, C., Bavoux, G., Burneleau, G., Eon, L. & Nicolau-Guillaumet, P. 1993. Lead poisoning in wild populations of Marsh Harriers *Circus aeruginosus* in the Camargue and Charente-Maritime, France. *Ibis* 135: 379–386.

Parr, R. 1992. The decline to extinction of a population of Golden Plover in north-east Scotland. *Ornis Scandinavica* 23: 152–158.

Parr, R. 1993. Nest predation and numbers of Golden Plovers *Pluvialis apricaria* and other moorland waders. *Bird Study* 40: 223–231.

Parr, S. 1994. Changes in the population size and nest sites of Merlins *Falco columbarius* in Wales between 1970 and 1991. *Bird Study* 41: 42–47.

Parslow, J.L.F. 1967. Changes in status among breeding birds in Britain in Britain and Ireland. *British Birds* 60: 2–47.

Parslow, J.F.L. 1973. *Breeding birds of Britain and Ireland*. Berkhamsted, T. & A.D. Poyser. 272 pp.

Parslow-Otsu, M. 1991. Bean Geese in the Yare Valley, Norfolk. *British Birds* 84: 161–170.

Partridge, J.K. 1989. Lower Lough Erne's Common Scoters. *RSPB Conservation Review* 3: 25–28.

Paterson, I.W. 1991. The status and breeding distribution of Greylag Geese *Anser anser* in the Uists (Scotland) and their impact upon crofting agriculture. *Ardea* 79: 243–252.

Pattersen, I. in press. Shelduck *Tadorna tadorna*. In: *The migration atlas: movements of the birds of Britain and Ireland*, by C.V. Wernham, M.P. Toms, J.H. Marchant, J.A. Clark, G.M. Siriwardena & S.R. Baillie. London, T. & A.D. Poyser.

Pemberton, J.E. 1997. *The Birdwatcher's Yearbook and Diary 1998*. Buckingham, Buckingham Press. 320 pp.

Penhallurick, R.D. 1969. *The birds of the Cornish coast, including the Isles of Scilly*. Truro, Bradford Barton. 200 pp.

Penhallurick, R.D. 1978. *The Birds of Cornwall and the Isles of Scilly*. Penzance, Headland Publications.

Percival, S., Bignal, E.M. & Moore, P. 1986. Whooper Swans in Islay & Kintyre – Autumn 1985. *The Third Argyll Bird Report*: 74–75.

Percival, S.M. 1991. The population structure of Greenland Barnacle Geese *Branta leucopsis* on the wintering grounds on Islay. *Ibis* 133: 357–364.

Percival, S.M. 1993. The effects of reseeding, fertilizer application and disturbance on the use of grasslands by barnacle geese, and the implications for refuge management. *Journal of Applied Ecology* 30: 437–443.

Percival, S.M. & Percival, T. 1997. Feeding ecology of barnacle geese on the spring staging grounds in northern Iceland. *Ecography* 20: 461–465.

Percival, S.M., Sutherland, W.J. & Evans, P.R. 1998. Intertidal habitat loss and wildfowl numbers: application of a spatial depletion model. *Journal of Applied Ecology* 35: 57–63.

Pettifor, R.A., Percival, S.M. & Rowcliffe, J.M. 1996. Greenland population of the barnacle goose (*Branta leucopsis*) – the collation and statistical analysis of data and Population Viability Analyses. *Scottish Natural Heritage Research, Survey and Monitoring Report*, No. 137. 45 pp.

Petty, S.J. 1998. *Ecology and conservation of raptors in forests*. London, The Stationary Office. (Forestry Commission Bulletin No. 118)

Phillips, R.A., Thompson, D.R. & Hamer, K.C. 1999. The impact of Great Skua predation on seabird populations at St Kilda: a bioenergetics model. *Journal of Applied Ecology* 36: 218–232.

Phillips, V.E. 1991. Pochard *Aythya ferina* use of chironomid-rich feeding habitat in winter. *Bird Study* 38: 118–122.

Pienkowski, M.W. 1984. Breeding biology and population dynamics of Ringed Plovers *Charadrius hiaticula* in Britain and Greenland: nest predation as a possible factor limiting distribution and timing of breeding. *Journal of Zoology, London* 202: 83–114.

Pienkowski, M.W. & Pienkowski, A.E. 1983. WSG project on the movements of wader populations in western Europe, eighth progress report. *Wader Study Group Bulletin* 38: 13–22.

Pierce, S. & Wilson, J. 1980. Spring migration of Whimbrels in Cork Harbour. *Irish Birds* 1: 514–516.

Piersma, T. 1986. Breeding waders in Europe: a review of population size estimates and a bibliography of information sources. *Wader Study Group Bulletin* 48, *Supplement*.

Piersma, T. 1994. *Close to the edge: energetic bottlenecks and the evolution of migratory pathways in Knots.* Doctoral thesis, Rijksuniversiteit Groningen, Netherlands. 366 pp.

Piersma, T. & Davidson, N.C. 1992a. eds. The Migration of Knots. *Wader Study Group Bulletin* 64, *Supplement*. 209 pp.

Piersma, T. & Davidson, N.C. 1992b. The migrations and annual cycles of five subspecies of Knots in perspective. In: The Migration of Knots. *Wader Study Group Bulletin* 64, *Supplement:* 187–197.

Piersma, T., Prokosch, P. & Bredin, D. 1992. The migration system of Afro-Siberian Knots *Calidris cantuus canutus*. In: The Migration of Knots. *Wader Study Group Bulletin* 64, *Supplement:* 52–63.

Pihl, S. & Laursen, K. 1996. A re-estimation of Western Palearctic wintering seaduck numbers from the Baltic Sea 1993 survey. *Gibier Faune Sauvage, Game and Wildlife* 13: 191–199.

Pirot, J.-Y., Laursen, K., Madsen, J. & Monval, J.-Y. 1989. Population estimates of swans, geese, ducks, and Eurasian Coot (*Fulica atra*) in the Western Palearctic and Sahelian Africa. In*: Flyways and reserve networks for water birds*, ed. by H. Boyd & J.-Y. Pirot. Slimbridge, IWRB Special Publication No. 9. pp. 14–23.

Player, P.V. 1971. Food and feeding habits of the Common Eider at Seafield, Edinburgh, in winter. *Wildfowl* 22: 100–106.

Pollitt, M., Cranswick, P., Musgrove, A., Hall, C., Hearn, R., Robinson, J. & Holloway, S. 2000. *The Wetland Bird Survey 1998–99: Wildfowl and Wader Counts.* Slimbridge: BTO, WWT, RSPB & JNCC. 236 pp.

Poole, A.F. 1989. *Ospreys*. Cambridge, Cambridge University Press.

Potts, G.R. 1998. Global dispersion of nesting hen harriers *Circus cyaneus:* implications for grouse moors in the UK. *Ibis* 140: 76–88.

Pounder, B. 1976. Waterfowl at effluent discharges in Scottish coastal waters. *Scottish Birds* 9: 5–36.

Prater, A.J. 1973. The wintering population of Ruffs in Britain and Ireland. *Bird Study* 21: 245–250.

Prater, A.J. 1976. The distribution of coastal waders in Europe and North Africa. In*: Proceedings of the 5th International Conference on Conservation of Wetlands and Waterfowl, Heiligenhafen 1974*, ed. by M. Smart. Slimbridge, IWRB. pp. 255–271.

Prater, A.J. 1981. *Estuary birds of Britain and Ireland.* Calton, T. & A.D. 440 pp.

Prater, A.J. 1989. Ringed Plover *Charadrius hiaticula* breeding population in the United Kingdom in 1984. *Bird Study* 36: 154–159.

Prater, A.J. & Davies, M. 1978. Wintering Sanderlings in Britain. *Bird Study* 25: 33–38.

Pressey, R.L. 1996. Protected areas: where should they be and why should they be there? In: *Conservation Biology*, ed. by I.F. Spellerberg. London, Longman. pp. 171–185.

Pressey, R.L., Humphries, C.J., Margules, C.R., Vane-Wright, R.I. & Williams, P.H. 1993. Beyond opportunism: key principles for systematic reserve selection. *Trends in Ecology and Evolution* 8: 124–128.

Prestrud, P., Black, J.M. & Owen M. 1989. The relationship between an increasing population of Barnacle Geese and the number and size of their colonies in Svalbard. *Wildfowl* 40: 32–38

Prestt, I. & Mills, D.H. 1966. A census of the Great Crested Grebe in Britain 1965. *Bird Study* 13: 163–203.

Pritchard, D.E., Housden, S.D., Mudge, G.P., Galbraith, C.A. & Pienkowski, M.W. 1992. *Important Bird Areas in the United Kingdom including the Channel Islands and the Isle of Man.* Sandy, RSPB/JNCC. 540 pp.

Prokosch, P. 1988. Das Schleswig-Holsteinische Wattenmeer als frühjahrs-aufenthaltsgebiet arktische watvogel-populationen am beispiel von Kiebitzregenpfeifer (*Pluvialis squatarola*, L. 1758), Knutt (*Calidris canutus*, L. 1758) und Pfuhlschnepfe (*Limosa lapponica*, L. 1758). *Corax* 12(4): 273–442.

Prys-Jones, R.P., Kirby, J.S. & Evans, A. 1988. *The role of the Uists as a late spring staging post for some Nearctic-breeding waders.* Tring, British Trust for Ornithology. (Research Report No. 38)

Prys-Jones, R.P., Underhill, L.G. & Waters, R.J. 1994. Index numbers for waterbird populations. II. Coastal wintering waders in the United Kingdom 1970/71–1990/91. *Journal of Applied Ecology* 31: 481–492.

Pulliainen, E. & Saari, L. 1992. Breeding biology of the Dotterel *Charadrius morinellus* in eastern Finnish Lapland. *Ornis Fennica* 69: 101–107.

Rae, R., Nicoll, M. & Summers, R.W. 1986. The distribution of Hardangervidda Purple Sandpipers outwith the breeding season. *Scottish Birds* 14: 68–73.

Ramsar Convention Bureau 2000. *Ramsar handbooks for the wise use of wetlands. No. 7. Strategic Framework and guidelines for the future development of the List of Wetlands of International Importance.* Ramsar Convention Bureau, Gland, Switzerland. 60 pp.

Rasmussen, J.F. 1999. *Birds of Danish SPAs: trends in occurrence.* Miljø- og Energiministeriet, Skov- og Naturstyrelsen. 119 pp.

Ratcliffe, D.A. 1972. The Peregrine population of Great Britain in 1971. *Bird Study* 19: 117–156.

Ratcliffe, D.A. 1976. Observations on the breeding of the Golden Plover in Great Britain. *Bird Study* 23: 63–116.

Ratcliffe, D.A. (ed.) 1977. *A Nature Conservation Review.* 2 volumes. Cambridge, Cambridge University Press.

Ratcliffe, D.A. 1990. *Birdlife of Mountain and Upland.* Cambridge University Press, Cambridge.

Ratcliffe, D.A. 1991. Upland birds and their conservation. *British Wildlife* 2: 1–12.

Ratcliffe, D.A. 1993. *The Peregrine Falcon.* Second Edition. London, T. & A.D. Poyser.

Ratcliffe, D.A. & Thompson, D.B.A. 1988. The British uplands: their ecological character and international signif-icance. In: *Ecological Change in the Uplands*, ed by M.B. Usher & D.B.A. Thompson. Oxford, Blackwell Scien-tific Publications. pp. 9–36.

Ratcliffe, N., Pickerell, G. & Brindley, E. 2000. Population trends of Little and Sandwich Terns *Sterna albifrons* and *S. sandvicensis* in Britain and Ireland from 1969 to 1998. *Atlantic Seabirds* 2(3): 211–226.

RBBP 1999. Honey Buzzards in Britain – an announcement by the Rare Birds Breeding Panel. *British Birds* 92: 345–346

Reay, P. 1988. *The Tamar Avocets.* Plymouth, Caradon Field and Natural History Club.

Rebecca, G.W. & Bainbridge, I.P. 1998. The breeding status of the Merlin *Falco columbarius* in Britain in 1993–94. *Bird Study* 45: 172–187.

Redpath, S.M. & Thirgood, S.J. 1997. *Birds of Prey and Red Grouse.* London, Stationary Office.

Reed, T.M. 1985. Estimates of British breeding wader populations. *Wader Study Group Bulletin* 45: 11–12.

Rees, E.C. 1987. Conflict of choice within pairs of Bewick's Swans regarding their migratory movements to and from the wintering grounds. *Animal Behaviour* 35: 1685–1693.

Rees, E.C. 1990. Bewick's swans: their feeding ecology and coexistence with other grazing Anatidae. *Journal of Applied Ecology* 27: 939–951.

Rees, E.C. 1997. Bewick's Swan *Cygnus columbianus bewickii*. In: *The EBCC Atlas of European Breeding Birds: Their Distribution and Abundance*, ed. by W.J.M. Hagemeijer, & M.J. Blair. London, T. & A.D. Poyser. Pp. 63

Rees, E.C. & Bacon, P.J. 1996. Migratory tradition in Bewick's Swans (*Cygnus columbianus bewickii*). *Gibier Faune Sauvage, Game and Wildlife* 12: 407–420.

Rees, E.C. & Bowler, J. 1997. Fifty years of swan research and conservation by The Wildfowl & Wetlands Trust. *Wildfowl* 47: 248–263.

Rees, E.C., Bowler, J.M. & Beekman, J.H. 1997a. *Cygnus columbianus* Bewick's Swan and Whistling Swan. *Birds of the Western Palearctic Update* Volume 1, No. 2: 63–74.

Rees, E.C., Kirby, J.S. & Gilburn, A. 1997b. Site selection by swans wintering in Britain and Ireland: the impor-tance of habitat and geographic location. *Ibis* 139: 337–352.

Rehfisch, M. & Austin, G. 1999. Ringed Plovers go east. *BTO News* 223: 14–15.

Rhijn, J.G. van 1983. On the maintenance and origin of alternative strategies in the Ruff *Philomachus pugnax*. *Ibis* 125: 482–498.

Rhijn, J.G. van 1991. *The Ruff.* London, T. & A.D. Poyser.

Richardson, M.G. 1990. The distribution and status of Whimbrel *Numenius p. phaeopus* in Shetland and Britain. *Bird Study* 37: 61–68.

Ridgill, S.C. & Fox, A.D. 1990. *Cold weather movements of waterfowl in Western Europe.* Slimbridge, IWRB. (IWRB Special Publication No. 13)

Ridgill, S.C., McKay, C.R. & Rees, E.C. 1994. *Greenland White-fronted Geese wintering on Islay.* Report to Scottish Natural Heritage. Slimbridge, WWT. 167 pp.

Risberg, L., Aulén, G., Bylin, K. & Tyrberg, T. 1990. *Sveriges fålgar.* Stockholm, SOF.

Roberts, G. 1991. Winter movements of Sanderlings *Calidris alba* between feeding sites. *Acta Oecologia* 12: 281–294.

Roberts, S.J., Lewis, M.S. & Williams, I.T. 1999. Breeding European Honey Buzzards in Britain. *British Birds* 92: 326–345.

Robinson, H.W. 1934. First nesting of Leach's Fork-tailed Petrel in Orkney. *Scottish Naturalist* (1934): 93.

Robinson, J.A. 1999. Migration and morphometrics of the Red-breasted Merganser *Mergus serrator* in northern Eurasia and the implications for conservation of this species in Britain and Ireland. *Wildfowl* 50: 139–148.

Rogaceva, H. 1992. *The Birds of Central Siberia.* Husum, Germany. 737 pp.

Rogers, M.J. & the Rarities Committee 1990. Report on rare birds in Britain in 1989. *British Birds* 83: 439–496.

Rose, P.M. 1995. *Western Palearctic and South-West Asia Waterfowl Census 1994.* Slimbridge, IWRB.

Rose, P.M. & Scott, D.A. 1994. *Waterfowl population estimates.* IWRB Special Publication 29. 102 pp.

Rose, P.M. & Scott, D.A. 1997. *Waterfowl population estimates. Second Edition.* IWRB Special Publication 44. 106 pp.

Rose, P.M. & Stroud, D.A. 1994. Estimating international waterfowl populations: current activity and future directions. *Wader Study Group Bulletin* 73: 19–26.

Rösner, H.-U. 1988. Following bird numbers when they keep changing: is monitoring of migratory waders possible? *International Wader Studies* 10: 94.

Rösner, H.-U. 1997. *Strategien von Zug und Rast des Alpenstrandläufers (*Calidris alpina*) im Wattenmeer und auf dem Ostatlantischen Zugweg.* PhD Dissertation, University of Frankfurt/M, Aachen, Shaker Verlag.

Rothery, P., Wanless, S. & Harris, M.P. 1988. Analysis of counts from monitoring Guillemots in Britain and Ireland. *Journal of Animal Ecology* 57: 1–19.

RSPB 1998. *Species action plan: Golden Eagle.* Sandy, RSPB.

RSPB 1999. *Birdcrime '98. Offences against wild bird legislation,* 1998. Sandy, RSPB.

RSPB, English Nature, British Reedgrowers Association, Broads Authority 1994. *Reedbed management for bitterns.* Sandy, RSPB. 8 pp.

Russell, I.C., Dare, P.J., Eaton, D.R. & Armstrong, J.D. 1996. *Assessment of the problem of fish-eating birds in inland fisheries in England and Wales.* Report to MAFF, Project No. VC0104. London, Directorate of Fisheries Research.

Ruttledge, R.F. & Ogilvie, M.A. 1979. The past and current status of the Greenland White-fronted Goose in Ireland and Britain. *Irish Birds* 1: 293–363.

Saari, L. 1995. Population trends of the Dotterel *Charadrius morinellus* in Finland during the past 150 years. *Ornis Fennica* 72: 29–36.

Sackl, P. 1993. A review of the current situation of Dotterel *Eudromias morinellus* in the central Alps of Austria. *Wader Study Group Bulletin* 71: 39–40.

Salmon, D.G. 1981. *Wildfowl and Wader counts 1980–81.* Slimbridge, The Wildfowl Trust. 51 pp.

Salmon, D.G. 1986. Mallard *Anas platyrhynchos.* In: *The Atlas of Wintering Birds in Britain and Ireland,* ed. by P. Lack. Calton, T. & A.D. Poyser. pp. 96–97.

Salmon, D.G. 1988. The numbers and distribution of Scaup *Aythya marila* in Britain and Ireland. *Biological Conservation* 43: 267–278.

Salmon, D.G. & Black, J.M. 1986. The January 1986 Whooper Swan census of Britain, Ireland and Iceland. *Wildfowl* 37: 172–174.

Salmon, D.G. & Moser, M.E. 1985. *Wildfowl and Wader Counts: The results of the National Wildfowl Counts and Birds of Estuaries Enquiry.* Slimbridge, The Wildfowl Trust.

Salomonsen, F. 1950. *Grønlands Fugle. The Birds of Greenland.* København.

Salomonsen, F. 1958. The present status of the Brent Goose (*Branta bernicla* (L.)) in Western Europe. *Videnskab Meddelelser Dansk Naturhistorisk Forenings, København* 120: 43–80.

Samigullin, G.M. 1998. Migration, breeding and population size of Curlew *Numenius arquata* in Orenburg Region, Russia. In: *Migration and international conservation of waders. Research and conservation on North*

Asian, African and European flyways, by H. Hötker, E. Lebedeva, P.S. Tomkovich, J. Gromadzka, N.C. Davidson, J. Evans, D.A. Stroud & R.B. West. *International Wader Studies* 10: 325–328.

Schafer, C.L. 1990. *Nature reserves. Island theory and conservation practice.* Washington and London, Smithsonian Institution Press. 189 pp.

Scott, D.A. 1980. *A preliminary inventory of Wetlands of International Importance for waterfowl in West Europe and Northwest Africa.* Slimbridge, IWRB. (IWRB Special Publication No. 2)

Scott, D.A. & Rose, D.A. 1996. *Atlas of Anatidae populations in Africa and western Eurasia.* Wetlands International Publication No. 41. Wageningen, The Netherlands.

Scottish Office 1995. *Circular No.6/1995. Nature Conservation: implementation in Scotland of EC Directives on the Conservation of Natural Habitats and of Wild Flora and Fauna, and the Conservation of Wild Birds: the Conservation (Natural Habitats, &c.) Regulations 1994.* Scottish Office, Rural Affairs and Natural Heritage Division.

Scottish Raptor Study Groups 1998. *The illegal persecution of raptors in Scotland.* Scottish Office Central Research Unit, Research Findings No. 17. Edinburgh, The Stationary Office.

Sears, J. & Avery, M.L. 1993. Population and productivity trends of Little Terns *Sterna albifrons* in Britain, 1969–89. *Seabird* 15: 3–16.

Sears, J., Ellis, P.M., Suddaby, D. & Harrop, H.R. 1995. The status of breeding Arctic Skuas *Stercorarius parasiticus* and Great Skuas *S. skua* in Shetland in 1992. *Seabird* 17: 21–31.

Selby, P.J. 1835. On the birds inhabiting the County of Sutherland, *etc. Transactions of the Natural History Society of Northumberland and Durham* 1: 288.

Self, M., O'Brien, M. & Hirons, G. 1994. Hydrological management of waterfowl on RSPB lowland wet grassland reserves. *RSPB Conservation Review* 8: 45–56.

Sellers, R.M. 1993. Racial identify of Cormorants *Phalacrocorax carbo* breeding at the Abberton Reservoir colony, Essex. *Seabird* 15: 45–52

Sellers, R.M. & Hughes, B. 1997. *Inventory of inland cormorant roosts and breeding sites in Great Britain.* (Contractor: WWT Wetlands Advisory Service) Unpublished report to Joint Nature Conservation Committee, Peterborough.

Serra, L., Magnani, A., Dall'Antonia, P. & Baccetti, N. 1997. Risultati dei censimenti degli uccelli acquatici svernanti in Italia, 1991–1995. *Biologia e Conservazione della Fauna* 101: 1–309.

Sharrock, J.T.R. 1976. *The Atlas of Breeding Birds in Britain and Ireland.* Berkhamsted, T. & A.D. Poyser.

Sharrock, J.T.R. & the Rare Breeding Birds Panel 1975. Rare breeding birds in the United Kingdom in 1974. *British Birds* 68: 489–506.

Shaw, G. 1995. Habitat selection by Short-eared Owls *Asio flammeus* in young coniferous forests. *Bird Study* 42: 158–159.

Shepherd, K.B. & Stroud, D.A. 1991. Breeding waders and their conservation on the wetlands of Tiree and Coll, Inner Hebrides. *Wildfowl* 42: 108–117.

Sheppard, R. 1993. *Ireland's Wetland Wealth: the birdlife of the estuaries, lakes, coasts, rivers, bogs and turloughs of Ireland.* Dublin, Irish Wildbird Conservancy.

Shimmings, P., Choudhury, S., Owen, M. & Black, J.M. 1993. *Wintering Barnacle Geese on the Solway Firth.* Slimbridge, WWT Report to SNH on the 1992–93 season.

Shrubb, M. & Lack, P.C. 1991. The numbers and distribution of Lapwings *Vanellus vanellus* nesting in England and Wales in 1987. *Bird Study* 38: 20–37.

Sim, I.M.W., Gibbons, D.W., Bainbridge, I. & Mattingley, W. 1999. *Status of the Hen Harrier* Circus cyaneus *in the UK and the Isle of Man in 1998.* Draft report to DETR/JNCC Raptor Working Group.

Sim, I.M.W., Gibbons, D.W., Bainbridge, I.P. & Mattingley, W.A. in press. Status of the Hen Harrier *Circus cyaneus* in the UK and the Isle of Man in 1998. *Bird Study.*

Siokhin, V., Chenichko, I. & Ardamatskaya, T. 1988. *Colonial-nesting waterbirds of the Ukraine.* Kiew, Akademia Nauk Ukrainiskoj SSR.

Sitters, H.P., Fuller, R.J., Hoblyn, R.A., Wright, M.T., Cowie, N. & Bowden, C.G.R. 1996. The Woodlark *Lullula arborea* in Britain: population trends, distribution and habitat occupancy. *Bird Study* 43: 172–187.

Skov, H., Durinck, J., Leopold, M.F. & Tasker, M.L. 1995. *Important Bird Areas for Seabirds in the North Sea including the Channel and the Kattegat.* Cambridge, BirdLife International. 156 pp.

Smart, M. (ed.) 1979. *Proceedings of the First Technical Meeting on Western Palearctic Migratory Bird Management:* Branta bernicla bernicla. Slimbridge, IWRB. 228 pp.

Smiddy, P. & O'Sullivan, O. 1998. The status of the Little Egret *Egretta garzetta* in Ireland. *Irish Birds* 6: 201–206.

Smit, C. & Piersma, T. 1989. Numbers, midwinter distribution, and migration of wader populations using the East Atlantic Flyway. In: *Flyways and reserve networks for water birds*, ed. by H. Boyd & J.-Y. Pirot. Slimbridge, IWRB. (Special Publication No. 9: 24–63)

Smit, C. & Wolff, W.J. (eds.) 1981. *Birds of the Wadden Sea*. Rotterdam, A.A. Balkema.

Snow, D.W. & Perrins, C.M. 1998. *The Birds of the Western Palearctic. Volume 1: Non-Passerines*. Concise Edition. Oxford & New York, Oxford University Press.

SOVON 1987. *Atlas van Nederlandse Vogels*. Arnhem, SOVON.

Sparks, T.H. 1999. Phenology and the changing pattern of bird migration in Britain. *International Journal of Biometeorology* 42: 134–138.

Spencer, R. & Hudson, R. 1979. Report on bird-ringing for 1978. *Ringing & Migration* 2: 161–208.

SRSG (Scottish Raptor Study Groups) 1998. *The illegal persecution of birds of prey in Scotland*. Edinburgh, The Stationary Office. (Scottish Office Central Research Unit, research findings, No. 17)

Stenning, J. 1994. *Moray Firth Monitoring: Winter 1993–1994*. Sandy, RSPB report.

Stone, B.H., Sears, J., Cranswick, P.A., Gregory, R.D., Gibbons, D.W., Rehfisch, M.H., Aebischer, N.J. & Reid, J.B. 1997. Population estimates of birds in Britain and in the United Kingdom. *British Birds* 90: 1–22.

Stone, C.J., Webb, A. & Tasker, M.L. 1995. The distribution of auks and Procellariiformes in north-west European waters in relation to depth of sea. *Bird Study* 42: 50–56.

Stone, C.J., Webb, A., Barton, C., Ratcliffe, N., Reed, T.C., Tasker, M.L., Camphuysen, C.J. & Pienkowski, M.W. 1995. *An atlas of seabird distribution in north-west European waters*. Peterborough, JNCC. 326 pp.

Stowe, T.J., Newton, A.V., Green, R.E. & Mayes, E. 1993. The decline of the Corncrake *Crex crex* in Britain and Ireland in relation to habitat. *Journal of Applied Ecology* 30: 53–62.

Strowger, J. 1998. The status and breeding biology of the Dotterel *Charadrius morinellus* in northern England during 1972–95. *Bird Study* 45: 85–91.

Stroud, D.A. 1992. *Greenland White-fronted Goose* Anser albifrons flavirostris *international conservation plan*. National Parks and Wildlife Service/International Waterfowl and Wetlands Research Bureau. Draft, 184 pp.

Stroud, D.A. 1994. Conservation and management of Dark-bellied Brent Geese in Britain. In: *Brent Geese in the Wadden Sea*, ed. by J. van Nugteren. *Proceedings of the international workshop 'Brent Geese in the Wadden Sea', Leeuwarden, the Netherlands, 22–23 September 1994*. LVBW, The Netherlands. pp. 29–34.

Stroud, D.A. 1996. Estimating international waterbird populations: use of Criterion 3(c). In: *Proceedings of the 6th Meeting of the Conference of the Contracting Parties to the Convention on Wetlands. Brisbane, Australia, 19–27 March 1996. Technical Sessions E and F*. Gland, Switzerland, Ramsar Convention Bureau. pp. 37–44.

Stroud, D.A. 1998. Reducing the impacts of forestry on peatlands. In: *Towards a Conservation Strategy for the Bogs of Ireland*, ed. by G. O'Leary & F. Gormley. Dublin, Irish Peatland Conservation Council. pp. 79–90.

Stroud, D.A. & Craddock, D.M. 1996. Chapter 5.12. Migrant and wintering waterfowl. In: *Coasts and seas of the United Kingdom. Region 13 Northern Irish Sea: Colwyn Bay to Stranraer, including the Isle of Man*, ed. by J.H. Barne, C.F. Robson, S.S. Kaznowska, J.P. Doody & N.C. Davidson. Peterborough, JNCC. pp. 140–145.

Stroud, D.A., Mudge, G.P. & Pienkowski, M.W. 1990a. *Protecting internationally important bird sites: a review of the EEC Special Protection Area network in Great Britain*. Peterborough, Nature Conservancy Council. 230 pp.

Stroud, D.A., Reed, T.M. & Harding, N.J. 1990b. Do moorland waders avoid plantation edges? *Bird Study* 37: 177–186.

Stroud, D.A., Reed, T.M., Pienkowski, M.W. & Lindsay, R.A. 1987. *Birds, bogs and forestry: the peatlands of Caithness and Sutherland*. Peterborough, Nature Conservancy Council. 121 pp.

Stroud, D.A., Condie, M., Holloway, S.J., Rothwell, A.J., Shepherd, K.B., Simons, J.R. & Turner, J. 1988. *A survey of moorland birds on the Isle of Lewis in 1987*. Peterborough, Nature Conservancy Council. (Chief Scientist Directorate Report No. 776. 91 pp.)

Stroud, J.M. 1985. The status of the corncrake on Islay 1985. *The Third Argyll Bird Report*: 89–92.

Stroud, J.M. 1992. *Statutory suspension of wildfowling in severe weather: review of past winter weather and actions*. Peterborough, JNCC. (Report No. 75)

Summers, R.W. 1994. The migration patterns of the Purple Sandpiper *Calidris maritima*. *Ostrich* 65: 167–173.

Summers, R.W. 1999. Numerical responses by crossbills *Loxia* spp. to annual fluctuations in cone crops. *Ornis Fennica* 73: 141–144.

Summers, R.W. & Mavor, R.A. 1995. Occupation pattern of lochs by Slavonian Grebes in Scotland. *Scottish Birds* 18: 65–70.

Summers, R.W. & Underhill, L.G. 1987. Factors related to breeding production of Brent Geese *Branta b. bernicla* and waders (Charadrii) on the Taimyr Peninsula. *Bird Study* 34: 161–171.

Summers, R.W., Ellis, P.M. & Johnston, J.P. 1988. Waders on the coast of Shetland in winter: numbers and habitat preferences. *Scottish Birds* 15: 71–79.

Summers, R.W., Jardine, D.C., Marquiss, M. & Rae, R. in press. The distribution and habitats of crossbills *Loxia* spp. in Britain, with special reference to the Scottish crossbill *Loxia scotica*. *Ibis*.

Summers, R.W., Strann, K.-B., Rae, R. & Heggås, J. 1990. Wintering Purple Sandpipers *Calidris maritima* in Troms county, northern Norway. *Ornis Scandinavica* 21: 248–254.

Summers, R.W., Underhill, L.G., Waltner, M. & Whitelaw, D.A. 1987. Population, biometrics and movements of the Sanderling *Calidris alba* in southern Africa. *Ostrich* 58: 24–29.

Summers, R.W., Underhill, L.G., Nicoll, M., Rae, R. & Piersma, T. 1992. Seasonal, size- and age-related patterns in body-mass and composition of Purple Sandpipers *Calidris maritima* in Britain. *Ibis* 134: 346–354.

Sunyar, C. & Manteiga, L. 1998. *Financial instruments for the NATURA 2000 NETWORK and nature conservation.* TERRA, Environmental Policy Centre, Madrid. 157 pp.

Swinburne, J. 1884. Notes on the island of Sula Sgeir or North Barra, and North Rona, with a list of birds inhabiting them. *Proceedings of the Royal Physical Society of Edinburgh* 8: 51–67.

Symonds, F.L., Langslow, D.R. & Pienkowski, M.W. 1984. Movements of wintering shorebirds within the Firth of Forth: species differences in usage of an intertidal complex. *Biological Conservation* 28: 187–215.

Tasker, M.L., Webb, A. & Matthews, J.M. 1991. A census of the large inland Common Gull colonies of Grampian. *Scottish Birds* 16: 106–112.

Taverner, J.H. 1970. Mediterranean Gulls nesting in Hampshire. *British Birds* 63: 67–79.

Taylor, B. & van Perlo, B. 1998. *Rails: A Guide to the Rails, Crakes, Gallinules and Coots of the World.* East Sussex, Pica Press.

Taylor, D.W., Davenport, D.L. & Flegg, J.J.M. eds. 1981. *The Birds of Kent – A Review of their Status and Distribution.* Kent, Kent Ornithological Society.

Taylor, M., Seago, M., Allard, P. & Dorling, D. 1999. *The Birds of Norfolk.* Sussex, Pica Press.

Taylor, R.J. ed. 1992. *Dorset Birds 1991.* Dorset, Dorset Bird Club.

Tempel, R. van den & Osieck, E.R. 1994. *Areas important for birds in the Netherlands. Wetlands and other areas of international or European importance for birds.* Technisch Rapport Vogelbescherming Nederland 13E, Vogelbescherming Nederland, Zeist. 126 pp.

Temple-Lang, J. 1982. The European Community Directive on bird conservation. *Biological Conservation* 22: 11–25.

Tharme, A.P., Green, R.E., Baines, D. & Bainbridge, I.P. in press. The effect of management for the sport shooting of red grouse on the population density of breeding birds on heather-dominated moorland. *Journal of Applied Ecology.*

Thingstad, P.G. 1994. Ærfugl *Somateria mollissima.* In: *Norsk Fugelatlas,* ed. by J.O. Gjershaug, P.G. Thingstad, S. Eldøy & J. Byrkjeland. Klæbu, Norsk Ornitologisk Forening. pp. 94.

Thom, V.M. 1986. *Birds in Scotland.* Calton, T. & A.D. Poyser.

Thomas, C.D. & Lennon, J.J. 1999. Birds extend their ranges northwards. *Nature* 399: 213.

Thomas, G.J. 1978. *Breeding and feeding ecology of waterfowl at the Ouse Washes, England.* PhD thesis, CNAA.

Thomas, G.J. 1980. The ecology of breeding waterfowl at the Ouse Washes, England. *Wildfowl* 31: 73–88.

Thomas, G.J. 1981. Field feeding by dabbling ducks around the Ouse Washes, England. *Wildfowl* 32: 69–78.

Thomas, G.J., Partridge, J., Wolstenholme, R.S., Richards, P., Everett, M.J. & Cadbury, C.J. 1982. The increase and feeding habits of Herring and Lesser Black-backed Gulls at Orfordness, Suffolk. *Transactions of the Suffolk Naturalist's Society* 18: 277–285.

Thompson, K.R. 1987. *The ecology of the Manx Shearwater* Puffinus puffinus *on Rhum, west Scotland.* PhD Thesis, University of Glasgow.

Thompson, K.R., Pickerell, G. & Heubeck, M. 1999. *Seabird numbers and breeding success in Britain and Ireland, 1998.* Peterborough, JNCC. (*UK Nature Conservation* No. 23)

Thompson, P.S. & Thompson, D.B.A. 1991. Greenshanks *Tringa nebularia* and long term studies of breeding waders. *Ibis* 133, *Supplement* 1: 99–112.

Thorup, O. 1998. Ynglefugelne på Tipperne 1928–1992. *Dansk Ornitologisk Forenings Tidsskrift* 92: 1–192.

Trolliet, B. & Girard, O. 1991. On the Ruff *Philomachus pugnax* wintering in the Senegal Delta. *Wader Study Group Bulletin* 62:10–12.

Tubbs, C.R. 1991. The population history of Grey Plovers *Pluvialis squatarola* in the Solent, southern England. *Wader Study Group Bulletin* 61: 15–21.

Tubbs, C.R. 1996. Estuary birds – before the counting began. *British Wildlife* 7(4): 226–235.

Tuck, L.M. 1972. *The Snipes: a study of the genus* Capella. Canadian Wildlife Service, Ottawa.

Tucker, G.M. & Heath, M. 1994. *Birds in Europe: their conservation status.* Cambridge, BirdLife International. 600 pp.

Tucker, G.M., Davies, S.M. & Fuller, R.J. 1994. *The ecology and conservation of Lapwings* Vanellus vanellus. Peterborough, JNCC. (*UK Nature Conservation* No. 9) 60 pp.

Tyler, G. 1994. Management of reedbeds for Bitterns and opportunities for reedbed creation. *RSPB Conservation Review* 8: 57- 62.

Underhill, M.C., Gittings, T., Callaghan, D.A., Hughes, B., Kirby, J.S. & Delany, S. 1998. Status and distribution of breeding Common Scoters *Melanitta nigra nigra* in Britain and Ireland in 1995. *Bird Study* 45: 146–156.

Underhill-Day, J.C. 1985. The food and breeding of Marsh Harriers *Circus aeruginosus* in East Anglia. *Bird Study* 32: 199–206.

Underhill-Day, J.C. 1998. Breeding Marsh Harriers in the United Kingdom, 1983–95. *British Birds* 91: 210–218.

Uttley, J., Monaghan, P. & Blackwood, J. 1989. Hedgehog *Erinaceous europaeus* predation on Arctic Tern *Sterna paradisaea* eggs: the impact on breeding success. *Seabird* 12: 3–6.

Venables, L.S.V. & Venables, U.M. 1955. *Birds and Mammals of Shetland.* Edinburgh and London, Oliver and Boyd.

Vessem, J. van & Kuijken, E. 1986. *Contribution to the determination of Special Protection Areas for Bird Conservation in Flanders (Belgium).* Unpublished report of Institute of Nature Conservation, Ministry of the Flemish Community. 94 pp.

Vickery, J.A., Sutherland, W.J. & Lane, S.J. 1994a. The management of grass pastures for brent geese. *Journal of Applied Ecology* 31: 282–290.

Vickery, J.A., Watkinson, A.R. & Sutherland, W.J. 1994b. The solutions to the brent goose problem: an economic analysis. *Journal of Applied Ecology* 31: 371–382.

Vïksne, J. 1997. *The bird lake Engure.* Jäna sëta, Riga, Latvia. 110 pp.

Village, A. 1987. Numbers, territory size and turnover of Short-eared Owls *Asio flammeus* in relation to vole abundance. *Ornis Scandinavica* 18:198–204.

Visser, M.E., van Noordwijk, A.J., Tinbergen, J.M. & Lessells, C.M. 1998. *Warmer springs lead to mistimed reproduction in great tits* (Parus Major). Proceedings of the Royal Society, London B. *Nature* 265:1867–1870.

Voous, K.H. 1960. *Atlas of European Birds.* Nelson, Amsterdam and London.

Voous, K.H. 1978. The Scottish Crossbill: *Loxia scotica. British Birds* 71: 3–10.

Walsh, P.M., Brindley, E. & Heubeck, M. 1995. *Seabird numbers and breeding success in Britain and Ireland, 1994.* Peterborough, JNCC (*UK Nature Conservation* No. 18). 51 pp.

Ward, S. & Hewitson, L. 1999. *Literature Review on the Slavonian Grebe.* Scottish Natural Heritage unpublished report.

Warnes, J.M. 1982. *A study of the ecology of the Chough* Pyrrhocorax pyrrhocorax *L. on the Isle of Islay, Argyll 1980–1981.* Unpublished report, University of Stirling. 68 pp.

Warnes, J.M. 1983. The status of the Chough in Scotland. *Scottish Birds* 12: 238–246.

Waters, R.J., Cranswick, P.A., Musgrove, A. & Pollitt, M. 1998. *The Wetland Bird Survey 1996–97: Wildfowl and Wader Counts.* Slimbridge: BTO, WWT, RSPB & JNCC. 176 pp.

Watson, A. 1989. Dotterel populations and spacing on three Scottish areas in 1967–1986. *Ornis Fennica* 66: 85–99.

Watson, A., Payne, S. & Rae, S. 1989. Golden eagles *Aquila chrysaetos*: land use and food in northeast Scotland. *Ibis* 131: 336–348.

Watson, A.D. 1986. Bean Geese in South-West Scotland. *Scottish Birds* 14: 17–24.

Watson, D. 1977. *The Hen Harrier.* Berkhamsted, T. & A.D. Poyser.

Watson, J. 1992. Golden Eagle *Aquila chrysaetos* breeding success and afforestation in Argyll. *Bird Study* 39: 203–206.

Watson, J. 1997. *The Golden Eagle.* London, T. & A.D. Poyser.

Watson, J. & Dennis, R.H. 1992. Nest-site selection by Golden Eagles in Scotland. *British Birds* 85: 468–481.

Watson, J., Rae, S.R. & Stillman, R. 1992. Nesting density and breeding success of Golden Eagles *Aquila chrysaetos* in relation to food supply in Scotland. *Journal of Animal Ecology* 61: 543–550.

Way, L.S., Grice, P., MacKay, A., Galbraith, C.A., Stroud, D.A. & Pienkowski, M.W. 1993. *Ireland's internationally important bird sites: a review of sites for the EC Special Protection Area network.* Report from JNCC to the National Parks and Wildlife Service of the Office of Public Works, Dublin and the Department of the Environment (Northern Ireland), Belfast. 231 pp.

Wernham, C.V., Armitage, M., Holloway, S.J., Hughes, B., Hughes, R., Kershaw, M., Madden, J.R., Marchant, J.H., Peach, W.J. & Rehfisch, M.M. 1999. *Population, distribution, movements and survival of fish-eating birds in Great Britain.* London, Department of the Environment, Transport and the Regions. 360 pp.

Wernham, C.V., Toms, M.P., Marchant, J.H., Clark, J.A., Siriwardena, G.M. & Baillie, S.R. in press. *The Migration Atlas: Movements of the Birds of Britain and Ireland*. London, T. & A.D. Poyser.

Westerhoff, D.V. & Tubbs, C.R. 1991. Dartford Warblers *Sylvia undata*, their habitat and conservation in the New Forest, Hampshire, England in 1988. *Biological Conservation* 56: 89–100.

Wetlands International 1999. *Report on the conservation status of migratory birds in the Agreement Area*. Report to first Meeting of the Parties to the African-Eurasian Waterbird Agreement, Cape Town, South Africa, 6–9 November 1999. 153 pp.

Whilde, A. 1978. A survey of gulls breeding inland in the west of Ireland 1977 and 1978 and a review of the inland breeding habit in Ireland and Britain. *Irish Birds* 1: 134–160.

Whilde, A. 1983. A repeat survey of gulls breeding inland in the west of Ireland. *Irish Birds* 2: 344–345.

Whilde, A. 1993. *Threatened mammals, birds, amphibians and fish in Ireland. Irish Red Data Book 2: vertebrates*. Belfast, HMSO. 224 pp.

Whitfield, D.P. 1997. Waders (Charadrii) on Scotland's blanket bogs: recent changes in numbers of breeding birds. In: *Conserving Peatlands*, ed. by L. Parkyn, R.E. Stoneman & H.A.P. Ingram. Wallingford, CAB International. pp. 103–111.

Whitfield, D.P. 2000. *Golden Eagle* Aquila chrysaetos *ecology and conservation issues*. Battleby, SNH.

Whitfield, D.P. in press. The status of breeding Dotterel *Charadrius morinellus* in Britain in 1999. *Bird Study*.

Whitfield, D.P., Duncan, K., Pullan, D. & Smith, R.D. 1996. Recoveries of Scottish-ringed Dotterel *Charadrius morinellus* in the non-breeding season: evidence for seasonal shifts in wintering distribution. *Ringing & Migration* 17: 105–110.

Whittingham, M.J., Percival, S.M. & Brown, A.F. 2000. Time budgets and foraging of breeding golden plover *Pluvialis apricaria*. *Journal of Applied Ecology* 37: 632–646.

Williams, G., Green, R., Casey, C., Deceuninck, B. & Stowe, T. 1997. Halting declines in globally threatened species: the case of the Corncrake. *RSPB Conservation Review* 11: 22–31.

Williamson, K. 1951. The Wrens of Fair Isle. *Ibis* 93: 599–601.

Williamson, K.W. 1958a. Bergmann's Rule and obligatory overseas migration. *British Birds* 51: 209–232.

Williamson, K.W. 1958b. Population and breeding environment of the St Kilda and Fair Isle Wrens. *British Birds* 51: 369–393.

Wilson, A., Vickery, J. & Browne, S. in press. The numbers and distribution of Lapwings *Vanellus vanellus* breeding in England and Wales in 1998. *Bird Study*.

Wilson, D.R. 1958. Leach's Petrels in Shetland. *British Birds* 51: 77–78.

Wotton, S.R. & Gillings, S. 2000. The status of breeding Woodlarks *Lullula arborea* in Britain in 1997. *Bird Study* 47: 212–224.

Yarker, B. & Atkinson-Willes, G.L. 1971. The numerical distribution of some British breeding ducks. *Wildfowl* 22: 63–70.

Yates, B., Henderson, K. & Dymond, N. 1983. *Red-necked Phalaropes in Britain and Ireland 1983*. Unpublished RSPB Report.

Zöckler, C. & Lysenko, I. 2000. *Water Birds on the Edge. First circumpolar assessment of climate change impact on Arctic Breeding Water Birds*. Cambridge, World Conservation Monitoring Centre. 23 pp.

Appendix 1

Glossary of terms used in this review

All-Ireland

All-Ireland comprises the whole of Ireland (Northern Ireland and the Republic of Ireland) (section 2.2).

All-Ireland population

The total population of a species occurring in the whole of Ireland (Northern Ireland and the Republic of Ireland). Standard 1% thresholds derived from all-Ireland population estimates are used for assessment purposes (section 4.2.1).

Area

Areas to be classified as SPAs should:

- be distinct in habitat and/or ornithological importance from the surroundings and have definable and recognisable character;

- provide the conservation requirements of the species in the season(s) and for the particular purposes for which they are classified.

(*see also 'Use' of areas*)

Biogeographical population

A group of birds which breed in a particular location (or group of locations), breed freely within the group, and rarely breed or exchange individuals with other groups. Standard 1% thresholds derived from biogeographical population estimates are used for assessment purposes (section 4.2.1).

Complementarity

The extent to which protected areas, within a network of protected areas, complement one another in the features (species or habitats) they contain.

Country

Country is taken to refer to either Scotland, Northern Ireland, Wales or England.

Density

The number of individuals of a species per unit area. In practice, a range of methods is used to assess numbers in SPAs, for example, breeding pairs and singing males.

Great Britain

Great Britain comprises Scotland, Wales and England, but excludes Channel Islands and the Isle of Man).

Great Britain population

The total population of a species occurring in Scotland, Wales and England, but excluding the Channel Islands and the Isle of Man. Standard 1% thresholds derived from Great Britain population estimates are used for assessment purposes (section 4.2.1).

Hectads

Ten-by-ten kilometre grid squares of the British and Irish national grids generally used as a framework for biological recording purposes.

International population

This term is used synonymously to refer to the relevant biogeographical population of the species concerned. It does not refer to the total world population for which the terms 'global population' or 'global numbers' are used where they are relevant.

Meta-population

A population of populations. A defined set of geographically separate populations with at least some exchange of individuals between the separate populations – in other words, systems of local populations connected by dispersing individuals.

Migratory

Article I(1)(a) of the Bonn Convention defines a migratory species as *"the entire population or any geographically separate part of the population of any species or lower taxon of wild animals, a significant proportion of whose members cyclically and predictably cross one or more national jurisdictional boundaries"*.

National

National is taken here to refer to the United Kingdom.

Natura 2000

The EU network of classified SPAs and Special Areas of Conservation (SACs) designated under Article 4 of the EU Habitats Directive (EEC/92/43). SACs are sites of European importance for habitats or species identified under the latter Directive.

Population viability

Populations which contribute most to population viability locally and as a whole may show one or more of the following attributes:

(1)   a level of recruitment into the breeding population that equals or exceeds immigration and mortality (averaged over a suitable period of time); and/or

(2)   small-scale population fluctuations around a stable population size; and/or

(3)   an area supporting a population of a species which enables its geographic range to be maintained on a long-term basis.

Best-available scientific data will be used to make such assessments.

Ramsar Convention

The informal name of the Convention on Wetlands of International Importance especially as Waterfowl Habitat (sometimes also known as the Convention on Wetlands). The Convention was adopted at a meeting of countries concerned with wetlands and waterfowl held in Ramsar, Iran in 1971 and was ratified by the UK in 1976.

Regular

The Conference of the Contracting Parties to the Ramsar Convention has defined the term 'regularly' as used in the Ramsar site selection criteria. This definition applies also to the SPA guidelines. A wetland regularly supports a population of a given size if:

(1)   the requisite number of birds is known to have occurred in two-thirds of the seasons for which adequate data are available, the total number of seasons being not less than three; or

(2)   the mean of the maxima of those seasons in which the site is internationally important, taken over at least five years, amounts to the required level (means based on three or four years may be quoted in provisional assessments only).

In some instances, however, for example species occurring in very remote areas or which are particularly rare, areas may be considered suitable on the basis of fewer counts.

Seabirds
In the context of the application of guideline 1.3, seabirds are defined as species within the families Procellariidae, Hydrobatidae, Sulidae, Phalacrocoracidae, Stercorariidae, Laridae and Alcidae.

Source
Area/local population, within which fecundity exceeds the sum of mortality and immigration, and results in a net emigration of individuals.

Special Protection Area (SPA)
An area classified under Article 4 of the Birds Directive.

SPA classification
The process of formally notifying SPAs to the European Commission.

SPA network
The total national (UK) network of all classified or proposed SPAs. It is the aggregate of many separate SPA suites.

SPA suite
Refers to those classified or proposed SPAs selected under Article 4 of the Bird Directive to fulfil relevant site-protection requirements for one particular species, sub-species or population.

Special conservation measures
Article 4.1 of the Birds Directive requires that "*special conservation measures*" are taken to conserve the habitat of species listed in Annex I of the Directive, to ensure their survival and reproduction in their area of distribution, in particular the classification of SPAs. Similar measures must be taken for regularly occurring migratory species, under Article 4.2.

Species range
The limits of a species' geographical distribution. Article 4 of the Birds Directive requires Member States to ensure the survival and reproduction of Annex I and regularly occurring migratory species "*in their area of distribution*". Article I of the Habitats Directive necessitates that, amongst other considerations, the "*natural range of the species*" be maintained for a species' status to be regarded as favourable.

United Kingdom
The United Kingdom comprises England, Northern Ireland, Scotland and Wales (but excludes the Channel Isles and the Isle of Man).

'Use' of areas
Article 4.2 of the Birds Directive requires special measures to be taken for migratory species at "*breeding, moulting and wintering areas and staging posts along their migration routes*". The boundary of each SPA is so determined that it delimits an area which provides the conservation requirements of the species in the season(s) and for the particular purposes for which it is classified.

Waterbirds

In the context of the application of guideline 1.3, waterbirds are defined as migratory species within the families Gaviidae, Podicipedidae, Phalacrocroracidae, Ardeidae, Threskiornithidae, Anatidae, Gruidae, Rallidae, Haematopodidae, Recurvirostridae, Burhinidae, Charadriidae, and Scolopacidae. The term waterfowl has the same meaning within the context of this review.

Appendix 2

Council Directive of 2 April 1979 on the conservation of wild birds (79/409/EEC)

COUNCIL DIRECTIVE
of 2 April 1979
on the conservation of the wild birds
(79/409/EEC)

THE COUNCIL OF THE EUROPEAN
COMMUNITIES,

Having regard to the Treaty establishing the European Economic Community, and in particular Article 235 thereof,

Having regard to the proposal from the Commission[1],

Having regard to the opinion of the European Parliament[2],

Having regard to the opinion of the Economic and Social Committee[3],

Whereas the Council declaration of 22 November 1973 on the programme of action of the European Communities on the environment[4] calls for specific action to protect birds, supplemented by the resolution of the Council of the European Communities and of the representatives of the Governments of the Member States meeting within the Council of 17 May 1977 on the continuation and implementation of a European Community policy and action programme on the environment[5];

Whereas a large number of species of wild birds naturally occurring in the European territory of the Member States are declining in number, very rapidly in some cases; whereas this decline represents a serious threat to the conservation of the natural environment, particularly because of the biological balances threatened thereby;

Whereas the species of wild birds naturally occurring in the European territory of the Member States are mainly migratory species; whereas such species constitute a common heritage and whereas effective bird protection is typically a trans-frontier environment problem entailing common responsibilities;

Whereas the conditions of life for birds in Greenland are fundamentally different from those in the other regions of the European territory of the Member States on account of the general circumstances and in particular the climate, the low density of population and the exceptional size and geographical situation of the island;

Whereas therefore this Directive should not apply to Greenland;

---

1   OJ No C 24, 1.2.1977, p.3; OJ No C 201, 23.8.1977, p.2

2   OJ No C 163, 11.7.1977, p.28

3   OJ No C 152, 29.6.1977, p.3

4   OJ No C 112, 20.12.1973, p.40

5   OJ No C 139, 13.6.1977, p.1

Whereas the conservation of the species of wild birds naturally occurring in the European territory of the Member States is necessary to attain, within the operation of the common market, of the Community's objectives regarding the improvement of living conditions, a harmonious development of economic activities throughout the Community and a continuous and balanced expansion, but the necessary specific powers to act have not been provided for in the Treaty;

Whereas the measures to be taken must apply to the various factors which may affect the numbers of birds, namely the repercussions of man's activities and in particular the destruction and pollution of their habitats, capture and killing by man and the trade resulting from such practices; whereas the stringency of such measures should be adapted to the particular situation of the various species within the framework of a conservation policy;

Whereas conservation is aimed at the long-term protection and management of natural resources as an integral part of the heritage of the peoples of Europe; whereas it makes it possible to control natural resources and governs their use on the basis of the measures necessary for the maintenance and adjustment of the natural balances between species as far as is reasonably possible;

Whereas the preservation, maintenance or restoration of a sufficient diversity and area of habitats is essential to the conservation of all species of birds; whereas certain species of birds should be the subject of special conservation measures concerning their habitats in order to ensure their survival and reproduction in their area of distribution; whereas such measures must also take account of migratory species and be coordinated with a view to setting up a coherent whole;

Whereas, in order to prevent commercial interests from exerting a possible harmful pressure on exploitation levels it is necessary to impose a general ban on marketing and to restrict all derogation to those species whose biological status so permits, account being taken of the specific conditions obtaining in the different regions;

Whereas, because of their high population level, geographical distribution and reproductive rate in the Community as a whole, certain species may be hunted, which constitutes acceptable exploitation; where certain limits are established and respected, such hunting must be compatible with maintenance of the population of these species at a satisfactory level;

Whereas the various means, devices or methods of large-scale or non-selective capture or killing and hunting with certain forms of transport must be banned because of the excessive pressure which they exert or may exert on the numbers of the species concerned;

Whereas, because of the importance which may be attached to certain specific situations, provision should be made for the possibility of derogations on certain conditions and subject to monitoring by the Commission;

Whereas the conservation of birds and, in particular, migratory birds still presents problems which call for scientific research; whereas such research will also make it possible to assess the effectiveness of the measures taken;

Whereas care should be taken in consultation with the Commission to see that the introduction of any species of wild bird not naturally occurring in the European territory of the Member States does not cause harm to local flora and fauna;

Whereas the Commission will every three years prepare and transmit to the Member States a composite report based on information submitted by the Member States on the application of national provisions introduced pursuant to this Directive;

Whereas it is necessary to adapt certain Annexes rapidly in the light of technical and scientific progress; whereas, to facilitate the implementation of the measures needed for this purpose, provision should be made for a procedure establishing close cooperation between the Member States and the Commission in a Committee for Adaptation to Technical and Scientific Progress,

HAS ADOPTED THIS DIRECTIVE:

Article 1
1. This Directive relates to the conservation of all species of naturally occurring birds in the wild state in the European territory of the Member States to which the Treaty applies. It covers the protection, management and control of these species and lays down rules for their exploitation.

2. It shall apply to birds, their eggs, nests and habitats.

3. This Directive shall not apply to Greenland.

Article 2
Member States shall take the requisite measures to maintain the population of the species referred to in Article 1 at a level which corresponds in particular to ecological, scientific and cultural requirements, while taking

account of economic and recreational require-ments, or to adapt the population of these species to that level.

Article 3

1. In the light of the requirements referred to in Article 2, Member States shall take the requisite measures to preserve, maintain or re-establish a sufficient diversity and area of habitats for all the species of birds referred to in Article 1.

2. The preservation, maintenance and re-estab-lishment of biotopes and habitats shall include primarily the following measures:

(a) creation of protected areas;

(b) upkeep and management in accordance with the ecological needs of habitats inside and outside the protected zones;

(c) re-establishment of destroyed biotopes;

(d) creation of biotopes.

Article 4

1. The species mentioned in Annex I shall be the subject of special conservation measures concerning their habitat in order to ensure their survival and reproduction in their area of distribution.

In this connection, account shall be taken of:

(a) species in danger of extinction;

(b) species vulnerable to specific changes in their habitat;

(c) species considered rare because of small populations or restricted local distribution;

(d) other species requiring particular attention for reasons of the specific nature of their habitat.

Trends and variations in population levels shall be taken into account as a background for evaluations.

Member States shall classify in particular the most suitable territories in number and size as special protection areas for the conservation of these species, taking into account their protection requirements in the geographical sea and land area where this Directive applies.

2. Member States shall take similar measures for regularly occurring migratory species not listed in Annex I, bearing in mind their need for protection in the geographical sea and land area where this Directive applies, as regards their breeding, moulting and wintering areas and staging posts along their migration routes. To this end, Member States shall pay particular attention to the protection of wetlands and particularly to wetlands of international importance.

3. Member States shall send the Commission all relevant information so that it may take appro-priate initiatives with a view to the coordi-nation necessary to ensure that the areas provided for in paragraphs 1 and 2 above form a coherent whole which meets the protection requirements of these species in the geographical sea and land area where this Directive applies.

4. In respect of the protection areas referred to in paragraphs 1 and 2 above, Member States shall take appropriate steps to avoid pollution or deterioration of habitats or any disturbances affecting the birds, in so far as these would be significant having regard to the objectives of this Article*. Outside these protection areas, Member States shall also strive to avoid pollution or deterioration of habitats.

Article 5

Without prejudice to Articles 7 and 9, Member States shall take the requisite measures to establish a general system of protection for all species of birds referred to in Article 1, prohib-iting in particular:

(a) deliberate killing or capture by any method;

(b) deliberate destruction of, or damage to, their nests and eggs or removal of their nests;

(c) taking their eggs in the wild and keeping these eggs even if empty;

(d) deliberate disturbance of these birds particularly during the period of breeding and rearing, in so far as disturbance would be significant having regard to the objec-tives of this Directive;

(e) keeping birds of species the hunting and capture of which is prohibited.

Article 6

1. Without prejudice to the provisions of paragraphs 2 and 3, Member States shall

---

* Article 7 (Directive 92/43/EEC) Obligations arising under Article 6 (2), (3) and (4) of this Directive shall replace any obligations arising under the first sentence of Article 4 (4) of Directive 79/409/EEC in respect of areas classified pursuant to Article 4 (1) or similarly recognized under Article 4 (2) thereof, as from the date of implementation of this Directive or the date of classification or recognition by a Member State under Directive 79/409/EEC, where the

prohibit, for all the bird species referred to in Article 1, the sale, transport for sale, keeping for sale and the offering for sale of live or dead birds and of any readily recognizable parts or derivatives of such birds.

2. The activities referred to in paragraph 1 shall not be prohibited in respect of the species referred to in Annex III/1, provided that the birds have been legally killed or captured or otherwise legally acquired.

3. Member States may, for the species listed in Annex III/2, allow within their territory the activities referred to in paragraph 1, making provision for certain restrictions, provided the birds have been legally killed or captured or otherwise legally acquired.

Member States wishing to grant such authorization shall first of all consult the Commission with a view to examining jointly with the latter whether the marketing of specimens of such species would result or could reasonably be expected to result in the population levels, geographical distribution or reproductive rate of the species being endangered throughout the Community. Should this examination prove that the intended authorization will, in the view of the Commission, result in any one of the aforementioned species being thus endangered or in the possibility of their being thus endangered, the Commission shall forward a reasoned recommendation to the Member State concerned stating its opposition to the marketing of the species in question. Should the Commission consider that no such risk exists, it will inform the Member State concerned accordingly.

The Commission's recommendation shall be published in the Official *Journal of the European Communities*.

Member States granting authorization pursuant to this paragraph shall verify at regular intervals that the conditions governing the granting of such authorization continue to be fulfilled.

4. The Commission shall carry out studies on the biological status of the species listed in Annex III/3 and on the effects of marketing on such status.

It shall submit, at the latest four months before the time limit referred to in Article 18(1) of this Directive, a report and its proposals to the Committee referred to in Article 16, with a view to a decision on the entry of such species in Annex III/2. Pending this decision, the Member States may apply existing national rules to such species without prejudice to paragraph 3 hereof.

Article 7
1. Owing to their population level, geographical distribution and reproductive rate throughout the Community, the species listed in Annex II may be hunted under national legislation. Member States shall ensure that the hunting of these species does not jeopardize conservation efforts in their distribution area.

2. The species referred to in Annex II/1 may be hunted in the geographical sea and land area where this Directive applies.

3. The species referred to in Annex II/2 may be hunted only in the Member States in respect of which they are indicated.

4. Member States shall ensure that the practice of hunting, including falconry if practised, as carried on in accordance with the national measures in force, complies with the principles of wise use and ecologically balanced control of the species of birds concerned and that this practice is compatible as regards the population of these species, in particular migratory species, with the measures resulting from Article 2. They shall see in particular that the species to which hunting laws apply are not hunted during the rearing season nor during the various stages of reproduction. in the case of migratory species, they shall see in particular that the species to which hunting regulations apply are not hunted during their period of reproduction or during their return to their rearing grounds. Member States shall send the Commission all relevant information on the practical application of their hunting regulations.

Article 8
1. In respect of the hunting, capture or killing of birds under this Directive, Member States shall prohibit the use of all means, arrangements or methods used for the large-scale or non-selective capture or killing of birds or capable of causing the local disappearance of a species, in particular the use of those listed in Annex IV (a).

2. Moreover, Member States shall prohibit any hunting from the modes of transport and under the conditions mentioned in Annex IV(b).

Article 9
1. Member States may derogate from the provisions of Articles 5, 6, 7 and 8, where there is no other satisfactory solution, for the following reasons:

(a) – in the interests of public health and safety,

  – in the interests of air safety,

  – to prevent serious damage to crops, livestock, forests, fisheries and water,

  – for the protection of flora and fauna;

(b) for the purposes of research and teaching, of re-population, of re-introduction and for the breeding necessary for these purposes;

(c) to permit, under strictly supervised conditions and on a selective basis, the capture, keeping or other judicious use of certain birds in small numbers.

2. The derogations must specify:

  – the species which are subject to the derogations,

  – the means, arrangements or methods authorized for capture or killing,

  – the conditions of risk and the circumstances of time and place under which such derogations may be granted,

  – the authority empowered to declare that the required conditions obtain and to decide what means, arrangements or methods may be used, within what limits and by whom,

  – the controls which will be carried out.

3. Each year the Member States shall send a report to the Commission on the implementation of this Article.

4. On the basis of the information available to it, and in particular the information communicated to it pursuant to paragraph 3, the Commission shall at all times ensure that the consequences of these derogations are not incompatible with this Directive. It shall take appropriate steps to this end.

Article 10

1. Member States shall encourage research and any work required as a basis for the protection, management and use of the population of all species of bird referred to in Article 1.

2. Particular attention shall be paid to research and work on the subjects listed in Annex V. Member States shall send the Commission any information required to enable it to take appropriate measures for the coordination of the research and work referred to in this Article.

Article 11

Member States shall see that any introduction of species of bird which do not occur naturally in the wild state in the European territory of the Member States does not prejudice the local flora and fauna.

In this connection they shall consult the Commission.

Article 12

1. Member States shall forward to the Commission every three years, starting from the date of expiry of the time limit referred to in Article 18 (1), a report on the implementation of national provisions taken thereunder.

2. The Commission shall prepare every three years a composite report based on the information referred to in paragraph 1. That part of the draft report covering the information supplied by a Member State shall be forwarded to the authorities of the Member State in question for verification. The final version of the report shall be forwarded to the Member States.

Article 13

Application of the measures taken pursuant to this Directive may not lead to deterioration in the present situation as regards the conservation of species of birds referred to in Article 1.

Article 14

Member States may introduce stricter protective measures than those provided for under this Directive.

Article 15

Such amendments as are necessary for adapting Annexes I and V to this Directive to technical and scientific progress and the amendments referred to in the second paragraph of Article 6 (4) shall be adopted in accordance with the procedure laid down in Article 17.

Article 16

1. For the purposes of the amendments referred to in Article 15 of this Directive, a Committee for the Adaptation to Technical and Scientific Progress (hereinafter called 'the Committee'), consisting of representatives of the Member States and chaired by a representative of the Commission, is hereby set up.

2. The Committee shall draw up its rules of procedure.

Article 17

1. Where the procedure laid down in this Article is to be followed, matters shall be referred to the Committee by its chairman, either on his own initiative or at the request of the representative of a Member State.

2. The Commission representative shall submit to the Committee a draft of the measures to be taken. The Committee shall deliver its opinion on the draft within a time limit set by the chairman having regard to the urgency of the matter. It shall act by a majority of 41 votes, the votes of the Member States being weighted as provided in Article 148 (2) of the Treaty. The chairman shall not vote.

3. (a) The Commission shall adopt the measures envisaged where they are in accordance with the opinion of the Committee.

   (b) Where the measures envisaged are not in accordance with the opinion of the Committee or if no opinion is delivered, the Commission shall without delay submit a proposal to the Council concerning the measures to be adopted. The Council shall act by a qualified majority.

   (c) If, within three months of the proposal being submitted to it, the Council has not acted, the proposed measures shall be adopted by the Commission.

Article 18

1. Member States shall bring into force the laws, regulations and administrative provisions necessary to comply with this Directive within two years of its notification. They shall forthwith inform the Commission thereof.

2. Member States shall communicate to the Commission the texts of the main provisions of national law which they adopt in the field governed by this Directive.

Article 19

This Directive is addressed to the Member States.

Done at Luxembourg, 2 April 1979.

For the Council

The President

J. FRANÇOIS-PONCET

Full lists of those species occurring on the various annexes of the Directive, which are modified from time to time, can be found on the World Wide Web at:

    http://europa.eu.int/comm/environment/
    nature/legis.htm

Modifications to the Directive

The various changes to the Directive since 1979 are listed below, together with a brief summary of their purpose.

Legal modification	Purpose of modification
Council Directive 79/409/EEC on the conservation of wild birds *(OJ No L 103, 25 April 1979, p. 1)*	Original text of the Directive
Council resolution of 2 April 1979 concerning Directive 79/409/EEC on the conservation of wild birds *(OJ No C 103, 25 April 1979, p. 6)*	Statement of intent by both the Council of Ministers and the Commission relating to actions to be taken under the Directive
Act concerning the conditions of accession and the adjustments to the Treaties – Accession of the Hellenic Republic *(OJ No L 291, 19 November 1979, p. 112)*	
Council Directive (81/854/EEC) of 19 October 1981 adapting, consequent upon the accession of Greece, Directive 79/409/EEC on the conservation of wild birds *(OJ No L 319, 7 November 1981, pp. 3–14)*	Added Greek vernacular names to the bird (sub-) species listed in Annexes I, II and III and indicated which species in Annex II/2 could be hunted in Greece
Act concerning the conditions of accession and the adjustments to the Treaties – Accession of the Kingdom of Spain and the Portuguese Republic *(OJ No L 302, 15 November 1985, p. 219)*	
Commission Directive (85/411/EEC) of 25 July 1985 amending Council Directive 79/409/EEC on the conservation of wild birds *(OJ No L 233, 30 August 1998, pp. 33–41)*	Modification of Directive following accession of Spain and Portugal as new Member States. Addition of further 70 species and sub-species to Annex I bringing total to 144 species and sub-species, *inter alia*, Merlin, Golden Plover, Hen Harrier
Council Directive 86/122/EEC of 8 April 1986 adapting, consequent upon the accession of Spain and Portugal, Directive 79/409/EEC on the conservation of wild birds *(OJ No L 100, 16 April 1986, pp. 22–25)*	Addition of Spanish and Portuguese bird names in the new official languages
Council Directive 90/656/EEC of 4 December 1990 on the transitional measures applicable in Germany with regard to certain Community provision relating to the protection of the environment *(OJ No L 353, 17 December 1990, p. 59)*	Article 5 of this Directive relates to the wild birds Directive
Council Directive 91/244/EEC of 6 March 1991 amending Council Directive 79/409/EEC on the conservation of wild birds *(OJ No L 115, 8 May 1991, p. 41)*	Amended Annexes I and III of the Directive bringing the Annex I total to 175 species and sub-species
Council Directive 92/43/EEC of 21 May 1992 on the conservation of natural habitats and of wild fauna and flora *(OJ No L 206, 22 July 1992, pp. 7–50)*	Modification of Article 4(4) of Birds Directive consequent upon Articles 6 & 7 of the Habitats Directive

Legal modification	Purpose of modification
Council Directive of 8 June 1994 amending Annex II to Directive 79/409/EEC on the conservation of wild birds (92/24/EC) *(OJ No L 164, 30 June 1994, p. 9–14)*	Amended Annex II/2 of the Directive
Act of accession of Austria, Finland and Sweden – Council Decision 95/1/EC *(OJ No L 1, 1 January 1995, p. 1)*	Modification of Directive following accession of new Member States. Amended Annex I (adding seven species, inter alia, Smew, Bar-tailed Godwit and Gyrfalcon), as well as Annexes II/2, Annex III/1 and Annex IV of the Directive as well as adding new bird names in new official languages
Commission Directive of 29 July 1997 Council Directive 79/409/EEC on the conservation of wild birds (97/49/EC) *(OJ No L 223, 13 August 1997, p. 9)*	Amendment of Annex I of the Directive by removal of Phalacrocorax carbo sinensis

Appendix 3

Population coverage of UK migratory birds and Annex I species within SPA suites

This Appendix lists all regularly occurring migratory species of birds in the UK (and species listed in Annex I of the Directive where these are regularly occurring within the UK). All solely resident species have been excluded from these tables (unless the UK breeding population is tiny in comparison with the number of immigrants).

Partial migrants (*i.e.* UK breeding species where a significant, but lower, proportion of birds cross national boundaries) have been indicated in the comment field. Annex I species are indicated by the lightest level of shading. Where these are not also migratory, this is shown in the status column.

Summary of bird species occurring in the UK SPA network in breeding and non-breeding seasons. Medium shading indicates that, although the species/population is present in the UK during the relevant season, no corresponding SPAs have been selected for the reasons outlined in the text (section 6) (*i.e.* present but no SPAs). Black indicates that, for some migrants, the species does not regularly occur in the UK during the season concerned (*i.e.* not present thus no SPAs). Light shading indicates that the species/population is listed on Annex I.

Name	Migratory status	Breeding season					Non-breeding season				
		Number of breeding sites in species' UK SPA suite	Total numbers in species' UK SPA suite (pairs)	% British (GB) breeding population	% all-Ireland breeding population in Northern Ireland	% international population	Number of non-breeding sites in species' UK SPA suite	Total numbers in species' UK SPA suite (individuals)	% British (GB) non-breeding population	% all-Ireland non-breeding population in Northern Ireland	% international population
Red-throated Diver	Partial migrant	10	395	42.2%		5.6%	1	88	1.8%		0.1%
Black-throated Diver	Partial migrant	11	95	61%		0.5%					
Great Northern Diver											0.2%
Little Grebe	Partial migrant						10	828	14.8%	7.6%	
Great Crested Grebe	Partial migrant	1	500		24.1%	1.0%	17	2,679	13.8%	43.2%	1.8%
Red-necked Grebe											
Slavonian Grebe	Partial migrant	6	37	53%		0.6%	3	31	7.8%		0.6%
Black-necked Grebe	Partial migrant										
Fulmar	Partial migrant	25	310,279	57.3%	4.7%	4.1%					
Cory's Shearwater											
Great Shearwater											
Sooty Shearwater											
Manx Shearwater		4	219,898	100%		82.9%					
Mediterranean Shearwater											
Storm Petrel		9	29,356	34.5%		11.4%					
Leach's Petrel		6	55,000	100%		5.8%					
Gannet	Partial migrant	10	197,127	98.1%		75.0%					
Cormorant	Partial migrant	7	2,316	29.5%	5.3%	5.6%	32	4,986	34.1%	5.3%	4.2%
Shag	Partial migrant	13	17,584	46.9%		14.1%					
Bittern	Partial migrant	5	18	90%		0.2%	10	50	50%		0.2%
Little Egret							3	225	45%		0.2%
Grey Heron	Partial migrant										
Purple Heron	Partial migrant										
White Stork											
Spoonbill											
Bewick's Swan							15	7,072	99.1%	5.4%	41.6%

Name	Migratory status	Breeding season					Non-breeding season				
		Number of breeding sites in species' UK SPA suite	Total numbers in species' UK SPA suite (pairs)	% British (GB) breeding population	% all-Ireland breeding population in Northern Ireland	% international population	Number of non-breeding sites in species' UK SPA suite	Total numbers in species' UK SPA suite (individuals)	% British (GB) non-breeding population	% all-Ireland non-breeding population in Northern Ireland	% international population
Whooper Swan							20	4,247	43.5%	18.5%	26.5%
Bean Goose							1	207	51.8%		0.3%
Pink-footed Goose							24	155,582	81.9%		69.1%
European White-fronted Goose							8	4,586	76.4%		0.8%
Greenland White-fronted Goose							12	8,243	58.9%		27.5%
Greylag Goose (Iceland population)							22	57,519	57.0%	18.2%	57.5%
Snow Goose	Partial migrant										
Barnacle Goose (Greenland population)							11	19,115	63.2%		49.8%
Barnacle Goose (Svalbard population)							2	13,821	100%		100%
Dark-bellied Brent Goose							19	93,677	93.7%		31.2%
Light-bellied Brent Goose (Svalbard population)							1	1,844	100%		54.2%
Light-bellied Brent Goose (Canada/Ireland population)							6	14,087		70.4%	70.4%
Shelduck	Partial migrant						32	65,472	83.7%	38.0%	21.8%
Wigeon	Partial migrant	2	80	27%		<0.1%	38	224,338	78.7%	3.1%	17.9%
Gadwall	Partial migrant	1	111	14.4%		1.1%	18	3,580	42.8%	25.9%	11.9%
Teal	Partial migrant						30	68,433	46.7%	4.8%	17.1%
Mallard	Partial migrant						14	29,137	4.9%	9.5%	0.6%
Pintail	Partial migrant						25	19,021	67.4%	2.4%	31.7%
Garganey		1	155	15.5%		1.6%					
Shoveler							26	3,582	34.6%	1.9%	9.0%
Red-crested Pochard	Partial migrant										
Pochard	Partial migrant						12	32,489	19.6%	59.6%	9.3%
Ring-necked Duck											
Ferruginous Duck											
Tufted Duck	Partial migrant						7	24,947	7.5%	51.2%	2.5%
Scaup							6	3,229	15.2%	51.9%	1.0%

Name	Migratory status	Breeding season					Non-breeding season				
		Number of breeding sites in species' UK SPA suite	Total numbers in species' UK SPA suite (pairs)	% British (GB) breeding population	% all-Ireland breeding population in Northern Ireland	% international population	Number of non-breeding sites in species' UK SPA suite	Total numbers in species' UK SPA suite (individuals)	% British (GB) non-breeding population	% all-Ireland non-breeding population in Northern Ireland	% international population
Eider	Partial migrant						8	9,023	11.5%	18.3%	0.5%
Long-tailed Duck							3	796	3.5%		<0.1%
Common Scoter	Partial migrant	2	37	49%		<0.1%	6	3,422	12.4%		0.2%
Surf Scoter											
Velvet Scoter							4	639	21.3%		<0.1%
Goldeneye	Partial migrant						15	12,788	25.6%	76.7%	4.3%
Smew											
Red-breasted Merganser	Partial migrant						15	2,177	19.3%	12.2%	1.7%
Goosander	Partial migrant						2	75	0.8%		<0.1%
Honey Buzzard	Partial migrant	1	2	13%		<0.1%					
Red Kite	Partial migrant	1	15	9.3%		<0.1%					
White-tailed Eagle	Not migratory										
Marsh Harrier	Partial migrant	10	116	74%		0.4%					
Hen Harrier	Partial migrant	14	229	47.4%		2.8%	20	244	32.5%		1.0%
Montagu's Harrier	Partial migrant										
Goshawk	Partial migrant										
Sparrowhawk	Partial migrant										
Buzzard	Partial migrant										
Rough-legged Buzzard							Largely resident on breeding areas (Appendix 5.5.1)				
Golden Eagle	Partial migrant	8	60	15%		1.2%					
Osprey		9	39	39%		0.8%					
Kestrel	Partial migrant										
Red-footed Falcon											
Merlin	Partial migrant	14	426	32.8%		4.2%	1	15	1.2%		<0.1%
Hobby											
Peregrine	Partial migrant	10	109	8.8%	1.9%	1.7%	Largely resident on breeding areas (Appendix 5.5.1)				
Capercaillie	Not migratory	6	364	16.5%		<0.1%					
Quail											
Water Rail	Partial migrant										
Spotted Crake		4	42	84%		<0.1%					
Corncrake		10	204	42.5%		0.2%					

Name	Migratory status	Breeding season					Non-breeding season				
		Number of breeding sites in species' UK SPA suite	Total numbers in species' UK SPA suite (pairs)	% British (GB) breeding population	% all-Ireland breeding population in Northern Ireland	% international population	Number of non-breeding sites in species' UK SPA suite	Total numbers in species' UK SPA suite (individuals)	% British (GB) non-breeding population	% all-Ireland non-breeding population in Northern Ireland	% international population
Moorhen	Partial migrant										
Coot	Partial migrant						6	19,050	13.7%	15.9%	1.3%
Crane											
Oystercatcher	Partial migrant	3	1,367	4.1%		0.5%	30	194,898	50.8%	23.7%	21.7%
Avocet	Partial migrant	6	549	92.7%		2.1%	16	2,225	100%		3.2%
Stone Curlew		3	184	97.9%		0.6%					
Little Ringed Plover											
Ringed Plover	Partial migrant	5	1,102	13.0%		6.9%	28	6,812	21.3%	5.1%	13.6%
Kentish Plover											
Dotterel	Partial migrant	8	469	55.8%		2.6%					
Golden Plover	Partial migrant	7	5,907	26.1%	3.0%	1.2%	22	67,233	21.8%	6.4%	3.7%
Grey Plover							28	38,842	90.0%	4.0%	25.9%
Lapwing	Partial migrant						38	212,834	9.8%	6.3%	3.0%
Knot							25	245,902	83.5%	10.3%	70.3%
Sanderling							11	3,535	15.4%		3.5%
Little Stint											
Temminck's Stint											
Pectoral Sandpiper											
Curlew Sandpiper											
Purple Sandpiper							3	1,973	9.3%		3.9%
Dunlin		8	6,812	74.0%		61.9%	38	420,758	77.8%	6.6%	30.1%
Buff-breasted Sandpiper											
Ruff		4	10	91%		<0.1%	8	316	45%		<0.1%
Jack Snipe	Partial migrant										
Snipe	Partial migrant						1	2,097	2.1%		0.1%
Woodcock	Partial migrant										
Black-tailed Godwit		2	42	100%		<0.1%	27	8,973	100%	3.2%	12.8%
Bar-tailed Godwit							23	39,386	70.1%	12.7%	39.4%
Whimbrel		1	65	12.3%		<0.1%	11	612	12.2%		<0.1%
Curlew	Partial migrant	1	3,930	11.9%		3.3%	25	50,206	38.3%	4.8%	14.3%
Spotted Redshank											

Name	Migratory status	Breeding season					Non-breeding season				
		Number of breeding sites in species' UK SPA suite	Total numbers in species' UK SPA suite (pairs)	% British (GB) breeding population	% all-Ireland breeding population in Northern Ireland	% international population	Number of non-breeding sites in species' UK SPA suite	Total numbers in species' UK SPA suite (individuals)	% British (GB) non-breeding population	% all-Ireland non-breeding population in Northern Ireland	% international population
Redshank	Partial migrant	4	1,660	5.4%		2.8%	36	56,739	48.4%	14.1%	37.8%
Greenshank	Partial migrant	2	408	28.3%		0.7%					
Green Sandpiper											
Wood Sandpiper		3	10	100%		<0.1%					
Common Sandpiper											
Turnstone							13	10,200	13.4%	7.1%	14.6%
Red-necked Phalarope		1	30	83%		<0.1%					
Grey Phalarope											
Pomarine Skua											
Arctic Skua		7	780	24.4%		2.6%					
Long-tailed Skua											
Great Skua		9	6,262	73.7%		46.0%					
Mediterranean Gull		5	23	74%		<0.1%					
Little Gull											
Sabine's Gull											
Black-headed Gull	Partial migrant	4	48,582	9.3%	61.3%	2.9%					
Ring-billed Gull											
Common Gull	Partial migrant	3	18,264	26.4%	7.3%	14.7%					
Lesser Black-backed Gull	Partial migrant	10	88,633	100%	11.6%	71.4%					
Herring Gull	Partial migrant	12	54,650	31.6%	9.0%	5.8%					
Iceland Gull											
Glaucous Gull											
Great Black-backed Gull	Partial migrant	6	4,457	23.4%		4.7%					
Kittiwake	Partial migrant	33	390,597	78.3%	13.6%	12.3%					
Sandwich Tern		16	11,440	72.2%	30.3%	8.7%					
Roseate Tern		7	56	88%	1%	3.2%					
Common Tern		22	6,993	46.2%	42.2%	3.6%					
Arctic Tern		17	17,124	37.9%	16.7%	1.9%					
Little Tern		27	1,616	67.3%		7.8%					
Black Tern											
Guillemot	Partial migrant	34	693,120	94.5%	27.4%	30.8%					

Name	Migratory status	Breeding season					Non-breeding season				
		Number of breeding sites in species' UK SPA suite	Total numbers in species' UK SPA suite (pairs)	% British (GB) breeding population	% all-Ireland breeding population in Northern Ireland	% international population	Number of non-breeding sites in species' UK SPA suite	Total numbers in species' UK SPA suite (individuals)	% British (GB) non-breeding population	% all-Ireland non-breeding population in Northern Ireland	% international population
Razorbill	Partial migrant	19	81,335	76.0%	26.2%	14.1%					
Black Guillemot	Partial migrant										
Little Auk											
Puffin	Partial migrant	21	470,284	c. 100%	11.7%	52.2%					
Stock Dove	Partial migrant										
Woodpigeon	Partial migrant										
Turtle Dove											
Cuckoo											
Snowy Owl	Not migratory										
Long-eared Owl	Partial migrant										
Short-eared Owl	Partial migrant	6	131	13.1%		1.0%					
Nightjar		10	1,785	52.5%		0.8%					
Swift											
Kingfisher	Not migratory										
Bee-eater											
Hoopoe											
Wryneck											
Short-toed Lark											
Woodlark	Partial migrant	7	1,102	73.4%		0.1%					
Skylark	Partial migrant										
Shore Lark											
Sand Martin											
Swallow											
Red-rumped Swallow											
House Martin											
Richard's Pipit											
Tawny Pipit											
Tree Pipit											
Meadow Pipit	Partial migrant										
Rock Pipit	Partial migrant										
Water Pipit	Partial migrant										

Name	Migratory status	Breeding season					Non-breeding season				
		Number of breeding sites in species' UK SPA suite	Total numbers in species' UK SPA suite (pairs)	% British (GB) breeding population	% all-Ireland breeding population in Northern Ireland	% international population	Number of non-breeding sites in species' UK SPA suite	Total numbers in species' UK SPA suite (individuals)	% British (GB) non-breeding population	% all-Ireland non-breeding population in Northern Ireland	% international population
Yellow Wagtail											
Grey Wagtail	Partial migrant										
Pied (White) Wagtail	Partial migrant										
Waxwing											
Fair Isle Wren	Not migratory	1	37	100%		100%	Largely resident on breeding areas (Appendix 5.5.1)				
Robin	Partial migrant										
Nightingale											
Bluethroat	Partial migrant										
Black Redstart	Partial migrant										
Redstart											
Whinchat	Partial migrant										
Stonechat											
Wheatear	Partial migrant										
Ring Ouzel											
Blackbird	Partial migrant										
Fieldfare											
Song Thrush	Partial migrant										
Redwing	Partial migrant										
Grasshopper Warbler											
Savi's Warbler											
Aquatic Warbler							3	47 (during passage)	70%		0.4%
Sedge Warbler											
Marsh Warbler											
Reed Warbler											
Icterine Warbler											
Melodious Warbler											
Dartford Warbler	Not migratory	6	1,681	c. 100%		<0.1%	Largely resident on breeding areas (Appendix 5.5.1)				
Barred Warbler											
Lesser Whitethroat											
Whitethroat											
Garden Warbler											

Name	Migratory status	Breeding season					Non-breeding season				
		Number of breeding sites in species' UK SPA suite	Total numbers in species' UK SPA suite (pairs)	% British (GB) breeding population	% all-Ireland breeding population in Northern Ireland	% international population	Number of non-breeding sites in species' UK SPA suite	Total numbers in species' UK SPA suite (individuals)	% British (GB) non-breeding population	% all-Ireland non-breeding population in Northern Ireland	% international population
Blackcap											
Pallas's Warbler											
Yellow-browed Warbler											
Wood Warbler											
Chiffchaff											
Willow Warbler											
Goldcrest	Partial migrant										
Firecrest	Partial migrant										
Spotted Flycatcher											
Red-breasted Flycatcher											
Pied Flycatcher											
Bearded Tit	Partial migrant										
Golden Oriole											
Red-backed Shrike											
Great Grey Shrike											
Woodchat Shrike											
Chough	Not migratory	9	112	32.9%		0.9%	8	241	35.0%		0.7%
Rook	Partial migrant										
Starling	Partial migrant										
Chaffinch	Partial migrant										
Brambling											
Serin											
Greenfinch	Partial migrant										
Goldfinch	Partial migrant										
Siskin	Partial migrant										
Linnet	Partial migrant										
Redpoll	Partial migrant										
Crossbill	Partial migrant										
Scottish Crossbill	Not migratory	5	295	98%		98%					
Common Rosefinch											
Lapland Bunting											

Largely resident on breeding areas (Appendix 5.5.1)

Name	Migratory status	Breeding season					Non-breeding season				
		Number of breeding sites in species' UK SPA suite	Total numbers in species' UK SPA suite (pairs)	% British (GB) breeding population	% all-Ireland breeding population in Northern Ireland	% international population	Number of non-breeding sites in species' UK SPA suite	Total numbers in species' UK SPA suite (individuals)	% British (GB) non-breeding population	% all-Ireland non-breeding population in Northern Ireland	% international population
Snow Bunting	Partial migrant										
Ortolan Bunting											
Little Bunting											
Reed Bunting	Partial migrant										

Appendix 4

Reference populations used in review

This Appendix summarises the standardised national (*i.e.* GB or all-Ireland) or biogeographic population figures used in this review. These data have been used to calculate proportions of Annex I or migratory species within SPAs. The proportion of such species' national or biogeographic population supported by the UK SPA network as a whole can therefore also be calculated. Usually only those species qualifying on at least one UK SPA are included.

Points regarding derivations:

(1) Where figures have been taken directly from source, these are shown as originally cited.

(2) Where population ranges have required the selection of a single population figure, the minimum has normally been taken.

(3) Where such ranges are small, typically those in Stone *et al.* 1997, the minimum figure is shown exactly.

(4) Where the range is large, typically in Rose & Scott 1997, the figure selected has additionally been rounded to produce a figure that can be more easily employed.

(5) The rounding of large population figures follows the methodology given in Stone *et al.* 1997, *e.g.* 1,000–10,000 to the nearest 100, 10,000–100,000 to the nearest 1,000, 100,000–1,000,000 to the nearest 10,000, *etc.*

(6) For a number non-Annex I migratory species, particularly ducks, breeding populations were derived by dividing the wintering figure by three, following Meininger *et al.* (1995) and Rose & Scott (1994,1997).

(7) Breeding populations of Guillemot, Razorbill and Puffin have been converted from individual birds to breeding pairs, using the methodology used by Lloyd *et al.* (1991).

(8) Biogeographical populations derived from data in Hagemeijer & Blair (1997) and defined here as 'European' exclude Turkey and European Russia.

F = individual females; M = calling males; P = pairs; I = individuals; A = individual adults

Species/ population	Season	GB population	GB population unit	GB population source	GB population derivation	All-Ireland population	All-Ireland population unit	All-Ireland population source	All-Ireland population derivation	Bio-geographic population and name	Bio-geographic population unit	Bio-geographic population source	Bio-geographic population derivation
Red-throated Diver	B	935	P	Gibbons et al. 1997	935–1,500 prs = minimum	<10	P	Gibbons et al. 1997		7,158 Europe	P	Hagemeijer & Blair 1997	7,158–10,502 = minimum
Red-throated Diver	W	4,850	I	Danielsen et al. 1993		1,000	I	Lack 1986		75,000 Europe/ Greenland	I	Rose & Scott 1997	
Black-throated Diver	B	155	P	Stone et al. 1997	155–189 prs = minimum					19,196 Europe	P	Hagemeijer & Blair 1997	19,196–26,548 = minimum
Black-throated Diver	W	700	I	Danielsen et al. 1993						120,000 Europe/ W Siberia	I	Rose & Scott 1997	
Great Northern Diver	W	3,000	I	Lack 1986		1,000	I	Lack 1986	1,000–1,500 = minimum	5,000 Europe (wintering)	I	Rose & Scott 1997	
Little Grebe	W	3,290	I	Kirby 1995		5,000	I	Sheppard 1993		550,000 W Palearctic	I	Rose & Scott 1997	100,000–1,000,000 Inds = midpoint
Great Crested Grebe	B	4,000	P	Gibbons et al. 1993	8,000 adults divided by two	2,074	P	Gibbons et al. 1993	4,150 adults divided by two	50,000 NW Europe	P	Rose & Scott 1997	Winter figure divided by three
Great Crested Grebe	P					3,060	I	Cranswick et al. 1997; Delany 1996b 1997/8	Average of September all-Ireland counts 1995–1997	150,000 NW Europe	I	Rose & Scott 1997	As for winter population
Great Crested Grebe	W	9,800	I	Kirby 1995		3,500	I	Delany 1996b		150,000 NW Europe	I	Rose & Scott 1997	
Slavonian Grebe	B	70	P	Ogilvie et al. 1996	70–78 prs = minimum					6,058 Europe	P	Hagemeijer & Blair 1997	6,058–9,268 = minimum
Slavonian Grebe	P	400	I	Stone et al. 1997	same as winter					5,000 NW Europe	I	Rose & Scott 1997	Same as winter
Slavonian Grebe	W	400	I	Lack 1986		30	I	Lack 1986	30–40 = minimum	5,000 NW Europe	I	Rose & Scott 1997	
Black-necked Grebe	B	23	P	Ogilvie et al. 1996	23–48 prs = minimum					33,000 W Palearctic	P	Rose & Scott 1997	Winter figure divided by three & rounded to nearest 10,000
Black-necked Grebe	W	120	I	Lack 1986						100,000 W Palearctic	I	Rose & Scott 1997	
Fulmar	B	539,000	P	Lloyd et al. 1991		31,300	P	Lloyd et al. 1991		7,540,000 N Atlantic	P	Lloyd et al. 1991	

Species/ population	Season	GB population	GB population unit	GB population source	GB population derivation	All-Ireland population	All-Ireland population unit	All-Ireland population source	All-Ireland population derivation	Bio-geographic population and name	Bio-geographic population unit	Bio-geographic population source	Bio-geographic population derivation
Manx Shearwater	B	220,000	P	Lloyd et al. 1991	220,000–250,000 prs = minimum	30,000	P	Gibbons et al. 1993	30,000–50,000 = minimum	265,100 World	P	Lloyd et al. 1991	Excludes birds now regarded as *P. mauretanicus* and *P. yelkouan*
Storm Petrel	B	85,000	P	Lloyd et al. 1991	20,000–150,000 inds = midpoint on JNCC Seabirds Team advice					257,000 World	P	Lloyd et al. 1991	135,000–380,000 = midpoint
Leach's Petrel	B	55,000	P	Lloyd et al. 1991	10,000–100,000 inds = midpoint on JNCC Seabirds Team advice					955,000 North Atlantic	P	Lloyd et al. 1991	780,200–1,130,600 = midpoint
Gannet	B	201,000	N	Stone et al. 1997						263,000 World	P	Lloyd et al. 1991	
Cormorant	B	7,000	P	Lloyd et al. 1991		4,700	P	Gibbons et al. 1993		41,200 *total P. c. carbo*	P	Lloyd et al. 1991	Total population of *P. c. carbo*
Cormorant	W	13,200	I	Kirby 1995		5,000	I	Way et al. 1993		120,000 NW Europe	I	Rose & Scott 1997	
Shag	B	37,500	P	Lloyd et al. 1991		8,800	P	Gibbons et al. 1993		125,000 N Europe	P	Lloyd et al. 1991	
Bittern	B	20	M	Stone et al. 1997						10,044 Europe	M	Hagemeijer & Blair 1997	10,044–11,669 = minimum
Bittern	W	100	I	Lack 1986	50–150 inds = midpoint on EN advice					25,000 Europe	I	Rose & Scott 1997	25,000–100,000 inds = minimum
Little Egret	P	800	I	BTO *in litt.* 1999						125,000 W Mediterranean	I	Rose & Scott 1997	100,000–150,000 = midpoint
Little Egret	W	500	I	BTO *in litt.* 1999						125,000 W Mediterranean	I	Rose & Scott 1997	100,000–150,000 = midpoint
Bewick's Swan	W	7,200	I	Kirby 1995		2,500	I	Way et al. 1993		17,000 W Siberia/NW Europe	I	Rose & Scott 1997	
Whooper Swan	P	5,600	I	Kirby 1995		10,320	I	Way et al. 1993		16,000 Iceland/ UK/Ireland	I	Rose & Scott 1997	
Whooper Swan	W	5,600	I	Kirby 1995		10,320	I	Way et al. 1993		16,000 Iceland/ UK/Ireland	I	Rose & Scott 1997	

Species/ population	Season	GB population	GB population unit	GB population source	GB population derivation	All-Ireland population	All-Ireland population unit	All-Ireland population source	All-Ireland population derivation	Bio-geographic population and name	Bio-geographic population unit	Bio-geographic population source	Bio-geographic population derivation
Bean Goose	W	450	I	Batten et al. 1990		[blacked out]				80,000 NE & NW Europe	I	Rose & Scott 1997	
Pink-footed Goose	W	192,000	I	Kirby 1995		[blacked out]				225,000 UK/ Iceland/ Greenland	I	Rose & Scott 1997	
European White-fronted Goose	W	6,100	I	Kirby 1995		[blacked out]				600,000 NW Siberia/NE & NW Europe	I	Rose & Scott 1997	
Greenland White-fronted Goose	W	13,700	I	Stroud 1992		14,000	I	Cranswick et al. 1999		30,000 total A. a. flavirostris	I	Rose & Scott 1997	Total population of A. a. flavirostris
Greylag Goose	W	100,000	I	Kirby 1995		3,800	I	Way et al. 1993		100,000 Iceland/ UK/Ireland	I	Rose & Scott 1997	
Barnacle Goose (Greenland)	W	31,009	I	Fox et al. 1990		7,500	I	Cranswick et al. 1997		32,000 Greenland/ Ireland/UK	I	Rose & Scott 1997	
Barnacle Goose (Svalbard)	W	17,450	I	Cranswick et al. 1997		[blacked out]				12,000 Svalbard/ UK	I	Rose & Scott 1997	
Dark-bellied Brent Goose	W	103,300	I	Kirby 1995		[blacked out]				300,000 total B. b. bernicla	I	Rose & Scott 1997	Total population of B. b. bernicla
Light-bellied Brent Goose (Canada)	W	[blacked out]				20,000	I	Way et al. 1993		20,000 Canada/ Ireland	I	Rose & Scott 1997	
Light-bellied Brent Goose (Svalbard)	W	2,430	I	Cranswick et al. 1992		[blacked out]				5,000 Svalbard/ UK/ Denmark	I	Rose & Scott 1997	
Shelduck	B	10,600	P	Gibbons et al. 1993		1,100	P	Gibbons et al. 1993		100,000 NW Europe	P	Rose & Scott 1997	Winter figure divided by three
Shelduck	W	73,500	I	Kirby 1995		7,000	I	Way et al. 1993		300,000 NW Europe	I	Rose & Scott 1997	
Wigeon	B	300	P	Gibbons et al. 1993	300–500 prs = minimum	[blacked out]				420,000 W Siberia/NW & NE Europe	P	Rose & Scott 1997	Winter figure divided by three & rounded to nearest 10,000
Wigeon	W	277,800	I	Kirby 1995		125,000	I	Way et al. 1993		1,250,000 W Siberia/NW & NE Europe	I	Rose & Scott 1997	
Gadwall	B	770	P	Gibbons et al. 1993		30	P	Gibbons et al. 1993		10,000 NW Europe	P	Rose & Scott 1997	Winter figure divided by three
Gadwall	W	8,200	I	Kirby 1995		600	I	Way et al. 1993		30,000 NW Europe	I	Rose & Scott 1997	

Species/population	Season	GB population	GB population unit	GB population source	GB population derivation	All-Ireland population	All-Ireland population unit	All-Ireland population source	All-Ireland population derivation	Bio-geographic population and name	Bio-geographic population unit	Bio-geographic population source	Bio-geographic population derivation
Teal	B	1,500	P	Gibbons et al. 1993	1,500–2,600 prs = minimum	400	P	Gibbons et al. 1993	400–675 = minimum	130,000 NW Europe	P	Rose & Scott 1997	Winter figure divided by three & rounded to nearest 10,000
Teal	W	135,800	I	Kirby 1995		65,000	I	Cranswick et al. 1999		400,000 NW Europe	I	Rose & Scott 1997	
Mallard	B	100,000	P	Owen et al. 1986	100,000–130,000 prs = minimum	23,000	P	Gibbons et al. 1993	By extrapolation from GB total	1,700,000 NW Europe	P	Rose & Scott 1997	Winter figure divided by three & rounded to nearest 100,000
Mallard	W	500,000	I	Owen et al. 1986		20,000	I	Way et al. 1993		5,000,000 NW Europe	I	Rose & Scott 1997	
Pintail	B	8	P	Ogilvie et al. 1996	8–42 prs = minimum	1	P	Gibbons et al. 1993		20,000 NW Europe	P	Rose & Scott 1997	Winter figure divided by three
Pintail	W	27,800	I	Kirby 1995		6,000	I	Cranswick et al. 1999		60,000 NW Europe	I	Rose & Scott 1997	
Garganey	B	15	P	Ogilvie et al. 1996	15–125 prs = minimum	1	P	Gibbons et al. 1993		670,000 W Siberia/Europe/ W Africa	P	Rose & Scott 1997	Winter figure (2,000,000) divided by three & rounded to nearest 10,000
Shoveler	B	1,000	P	Gibbons et al. 1993	1,000–1,500 prs = minimum	100	P	Gibbons et al. 1993		13,300 NW & C Europe	P	Rose & Scott 1997	Winter figure divided by three & rounded to nearest 100
Shoveler	W	10,000	I	Kirby 1995		6,500	I	Way et al. 1993		40,000 NW & C Europe	I	Rose & Scott 1997	
Pochard	B	251	P	Ogilvie et al. 1996	251–406 prs = minimum	30	P	Gibbons et al. 1993		120,000 NW & NE Europe	P	Rose & Scott 1997	Winter figure divided by three & rounded to nearest 10,000
Pochard	W	43,700	I	Kirby 1995		40,000	I	Way et al. 1993		350,000 NW & NE Europe	I	Rose & Scott 1997	
Tufted Duck	W	60,600	I	Kirby 1995		40,000	I	Way et al. 1993		1,000,000 NW Europe	I	Rose & Scott 1997	
Scaup	W	11,000	I	Kirby et al. 1993		3,000	I	Delany 1996b		310,000 N & W Europe	I	Rose & Scott 1997	
Eider	B	31,000	P	Gibbons et al. 1993	31,000–32,000 females = minimum pairs	600	P	Gibbons et al. 1993		500,000 Europe	P	Rose & Scott 1997	Winter figure divided by three

Species/population	Season	GB population	GB population unit	GB population source	GB population derivation	All-Ireland population	All-Ireland population unit	All-Ireland population source	All-Ireland population derivation	Bio-geographic population and name	Bio-geographic population unit	Bio-geographic population source	Bio-geographic population derivation
Eider	W	77,500	I	Kirby et al. 1993		2,000	I	Cranswick et al. 1999		1,500,000 W European S. m. mollissima	I	Derived from Rose & Scott 1997	Combined totals of the Britain and Ireland, and Baltic, Denmark & Netherlands wintering groups 1,415,000–1,775,000
Long-tailed Duck	W	23,500	I	Kirby et al. 1993		Unknown	I	Delany 1996	Threshold of 50 adopted	150,000 Iceland/Greenland	I	Rose & Scott 1997	
Common Scoter	B	75	F	Underhill et al. 1998		95	F	Underhill et al. 1998		530,000 W Siberia/N & W Europe/NW Africa	P	Rose & Scott 1997	Winter figure divided by three & rounded to nearest 10,000
Common Scoter	W	27,350	I	Kirby et al. 1993	Corrected from published paper to exclude Irish totals	4,000	I	Cranswick et al. 1999		1,600,000 W Siberia/N & W Europe/NW Africa	I	Rose & Scott 1997	
Velvet Scoter	W	3,000	I	Kirby et al. 1993						1,000,000 W Siberia/N Europe	I	Rose & Scott 1997	
Goldeneye	B	83	P	Ogilvie et al. 1996	83–109 prs = minimum					100,000 NW & C Europe	P	Rose & Scott 1997	Winter figure divided by three
Goldeneye	W	17,000	I	Kirby 1995		11,000	I	Way et al. 1993		300,000 NW & C Europe	I	Rose & Scott 1997	
Smew	W	250	I	Lack 1986		<10	I	Delany 1996a, 1996b		25,000 NW & C Europe	I	Rose & Scott 1997	25,000–30,000 inds = minimum
Red-breasted Merganser	W	10,000	I	Kirby et al. 1993		2,000	I	Cranswick et al. 1999		125,000 NW & C Europe	I	Rose & Scott 1997	
Goosander	W	8,900	I	Kirby 1995						200,000 NW & C Europe	I	Rose & Scott 1997	
Honey Buzzard	B	16	P	DETR/JNCC Raptor Working Group 1998						41,200 Europe	P	Hagemeijer & Blair 1997	41,200–48,677 = minimum
Red Kite	B	161	P	DETR/JNCC Raptor Working Group 1998						17,394 Europe	P	Hagemeijer & Blair 1997	17,394–28,185 = minimum

Species/ population	Season	GB population	GB population unit	GB population source	GB population derivation	All-Ireland population	All-Ireland population unit	All-Ireland population source	All-Ireland population derivation	Bio-geographic population and name	Bio-geographic population unit	Bio-geographic population source	Bio-geographic population derivation
Red Kite	W	1,320	I	CCW unpublished	1998					52,182 Europe	I	Hagemeijer & Blair 1997	Breeding population × 3
Marsh Harrier	B	157	F	Stone et al. 1997	157–160 prs = minimum					25,955 Europe	P	Hagemeijer & Blair 1997	25,955–34,675 = minimum
Hen Harrier	B	483	P	RSPB unpublished 1998		180	P	Gibbons et al. 1993		8,332 Europe	P	Hagemeijer & Blair 1997	8,332–10,840 = minimum
Hen Harrier	W	750	I	Lack 1986		540	I	Gibbons et al. 1993	Breeding population × 3	24,996 Europe	I	Hagemeijer & Blair 1997	Breeding population × 3
Montagu's Harrier	B	11	P	DETR/ JNCC Raptor Working Group 1998	11–21 = minimum					6,976 Europe	P	Hagemeijer & Blair 1997	6,976–9,610 = minimum
Golden Eagle	B	400	P	DETR/ JNCC Raptor Working Group 1998	400–450 = minimum					5,239 Europe	P	Hagemeijer & Blair 1997	5,239–5,616 = minimum
Osprey	B	99	P	Stone et al. 1997						4,732 Europe	P	Hagemeijer & Blair 1997	4,732–5,249 = minimum
Merlin	B	1,300	P	Rebecca & Bainbridge 1998		110	P	Gibbons et al. 1993	110–130 = minimum	10,200 Europe	P	Hagemeijer & Blair 1997	10,166–16,612 = minimum
Merlin	W	1,300	I	Stroud et al. 1990	1,500–2,500 = minimum	416	I	Derived from data in Lack 1986 (2–3 birds/ occupied square)	416–624 = minimum	30,600 Europe	I	From Hagemeijer & Blair 1997	Breeding estimate × 3
Hobby	B	500	P	Gibbons et al. 1993	500–900 prs = minimum					20,000 Europe	P	Hagemeijer & Blair 1997	19,720–22,799 = rounded minimum

Species/ population	Season	GB population	GB population unit	GB population source	GB population derivation	All-Ireland population	All-Ireland population unit	All-Ireland population source	All-Ireland population derivation	Bio-geographic population name	Bio-geographic population unit	Bio-geographic population source	Bio-geographic population derivation
Peregrine	B	1,167	P	DETR/ JNCC Raptor Working Group 2000		365	P	Gibbons et al. 1993		5,633 Europe	P	Hagemeijer & Blair 1997	Hagemeijer 5,633–6,075 = minimum
Capercaillie	B	2,200	IA	Catt et al. 1994		■				209,500 Europe	P	Hagemeijer & Blair 1997	Hagemeijer 209,405–296,085 = rounded minimum
Quail	B	515	M	Ogilvie et al. 1998	Total of probable & possible pairs	<20	M	Gibbons et al. 1993	In years without invasions	640,000 Europe	P	Hagemeijer & Blair 1997	Hagemeijer 641,525–876,497 = rounded minimum
Water Rail	B	450	P	Gibbons et al. 1993	450–900 = minimum	850	P	Gibbons et al. 1993	850–1,700 = minimum	129,994 Europe	P	Hagemeijer & Blair 1997	Hagemeijer 129,994–239,718 = minimum
Water Rail	W	Unknown	I			Unknown	I			550,000 Europe	I	Rose & Scott 1997	100,000–1,000,000 = midpoint
Spotted Crake	B	50	M	JNCC unpublished		■				48,800 Europe	P	Hagemeijer & Blair 1997	Hagemeijer 48,786–67,083 = rounded minimum
Corncrake	B	480	M	Green 1995		174	M	Green et al. 1997a	1993 data	87,500 Europe	M	Hagemeijer & Blair 1997	Hagemeijer 87,470–96,920 = rounded minimum
Coot	W	114,100	I	Kirby 1995		25,000	I	Cranswick et al. 1999		1,500,000 NW Europe	I	Rose & Scott 1997	
Oystercatcher	B	33,000	P	Piersma 1986	33,000 prs = minimum	3,000	P	Piersma 1986	3,000–4,000 = minimum	290,000 Europe/ W Africa	P	Rose & Scott 1997	Winter figure divided by three & rounded to nearest 10,000
Oystercatcher	W	359,000	I	Cayford & Waters 1996		50,000	I	Cranswick et al. 1999		874,000 Europe/ W Africa (East Atlantic Flyway)	I	Rose & Scott 1997	
Black-winged Stilt	B	1	P	Batten et al. 1990						15,400 Europe	P	Hagemeijer & Blair 1997	Hagemeijer 15,382–16,750 = rounded minimum
Avocet	B	592	P	Ogilvie et al. 1996	592–654 = minimum					26,800 Europe	P	Hagemeijer & Blair 1997	Hagemeijer 26,762–29,436 = minimum
Avocet	P	1,700	I	Stone et al. 1997						67,000 Europe/ NW Africa	I	Rose & Scott 1997	
Avocet	W	1,270	I	Cayford & Waters 1996						67,000 Europe/ NW Africa	I	Rose & Scott 1997	

Species/ population	Season	GB population	GB population unit	GB population source	GB population derivation	All-Ireland population	All-Ireland population unit	All-Ireland population source	All-Ireland population derivation	Bio-geographic population and name	Bio-geographic population unit	Bio-geographic population source	Bio-geographic population derivation
Stone Curlew	B	188	P	English Nature unpublished	1998 count					32,690 Europe	P	Hagemeijer & Blair 1997	Hagemeijer 32,690–45.704 = minimum
Ringed Plover	B	8,500	P	Prater 1989		1,250	P	Gibbons et al. 1993		16,000 Europe/ NW Africa	I	Rose & Scott 1997	Winter figure divided by three & rounded to nearest 1,000
Ringed Plover	P	30,000	I	Stone et al. 1997		Unknown				47,500 Europe/ NW Africa	I	Rose & Scott 1997	As from winter figure
Ringed Plover	W	28,600	I	Cayford & Waters 1996		12,500	I	Way et al. 1993		47,500 Europe/ NW Africa	I	Rose & Scott 1997	
Dotterel	B	840	P	Galbraith et al. 1993	840–950 = minimum					17,922 Europe	P	Hagemeijer & Blair 1997	Hagemeijer 17,922–39,136 = minimum
Golden Plover	B	22,600	P	Gibbons et al. 1993		400	P	Gibbons et al. 1993		474,900 Europe	P	Hagemeijer & Blair 1997	Hagemeijer 474,920–621,757 = minimum
Golden Plover	W	250,000	I	Cayford & Waters 1996		200,000	I	Way et al. 1993	>200,000 inds = minimum	1,800,000 NW Europe	I	Rose & Scott 1997	
Grey Plover	W	43,200	I	Cayford & Waters 1996		4,000	I	Cranswick et al. 1999		168,000 East Atlantic	I	Rose & Scott 1997	
Lapwing	B	190,000	P	Shrubb & Lack 1991; Thom 1986	190,000– 240,000 = minimum	21,500	P	Gibbons et al. 1993		2,300,000 Europe/ West Africa	P	Rose & Scott 1997	Winter figure divided by three & rounded to nearest 100,000
Lapwing	W	1,500,000	I	Cayford & Waters 1996	1,500,000– 2,000,000 = minimum	250,000	I	Cranswick et al. 1999		7,000,000 Europe/West Africa	I	Rose & Scott 1997	
Knot	W	291,000	I	Cayford & Waters 1996	= C. c. islandica	37,500	I	Way et al. 1993	= C. c. islandica	345,000 W Europe/Canada	I	Rose & Scott 1997	Total population of C. c. islandica
Sanderling	P	30,000	P	Cranswick et al. 1997		Unknown				123,000 East Atlantic	I	Rose & Scott 1997	
Sanderling	W	23,200	I	Cayford & Waters 1996		3,500	I	Cranswick et al. 1999		123,000 East Atlantic	I	Rose & Scott 1997	
Purple Sandpiper	B	2	P	Ogilvie et al. 1996						17,000 East Atlantic	P	Rose & Scott 1997	Winter figure divided by three & rounded to nearest 1,000

Species/ population	Season	GB population	GB population unit	GB population source	GB population derivation	All-Ireland population	All-Ireland population unit	All-Ireland population source	All-Ireland population derivation	Bio-geographic population and name	Bio-geographic population unit	Bio-geographic population source	Bio-geographic population derivation
Purple Sandpiper	W	21,300	I	Cayford & Waters 1996		1,000	I	Cranswick et al. 1999		50,500 East Atlantic	I	Rose & Scott 1997	
Dunlin	B	9,150	P	Reed 1985; Stroud et al. 1987	9,150–9,900 prs = minimum = C. a. schinzii	175	P	Hutchinson 1989	= C. a. schinzii	11,000 temperate European C.a. schinzii	P	Stroud et al. 1990	Temperate European figure (11,158 prs) extrapolated from British breeding popn figures & rounded to nearest 1,000
Dunlin	W	532,000	I	Cayford & Waters 1996		125,000	I	Cranswick et al. 1999		1,373,000 Northern Siberia/ Europe/ Western Africa	I	Rose & Scott 1997	
Ruff	B	11	N	Ogilvie et al. 1996	2–24 = midpoint on JNCC advice					105,700 Europe	P	Hagemeijer & Blair 1997	105,655–139,209 = rounded minimum
Ruff	P	1,100	I	Stone et al. 1997						1,000,000 West Africa	I	Rose & Scott 1997	>1,000,000 = minimum
Ruff	W	700	I	Cayford & Waters 1996		<20	I	Delany 1996		1,000,000 West Africa	I	Rose & Scott 1997	>1,000,000 = minimum
Snipe (G. g. gallinago)	B	55,000	P	Gibbons et al. 1993		10,000	P	Piersma 1986	minimum estimate	862,000 Europe	P	Hagemeijer & Blair 1997	861,593–990,503 = rounded minimum
Snipe (G. g. faeroeensis)	B	6,900	P	BTO in litt. 2001						250,000 total G. g. faeroeensis	P	Rose & Scott 1997	750,000 divided by three Total population of G. g. faeroeensis
Snipe	W	100,000	I	Cayford & Waters 1996	>100,000 = minimum	Unknown				2,000,000 Europe/ West Africa	I	Rose & Scott 1997	>2,000,000 = minimum
Black-tailed Godwit (L. l. limosa)	B	34	P	Ogilvie et al. 1996	34–41 pairs = minimum					120,000 W Africa/W Europe	P	Rose & Scott 1997	350,000 divided by three & rounded to nearest 10,000
Black-tailed Godwit (L. l. islandica)	B	?	P			2	P	Gibbons et al. 1993		5,000 Iceland	P	Hagemeijer & Blair 1997	5,000–15,000 = minimum
Black-tailed Godwit (L. l. islandica)	W	7,410	I	Cayford & Waters 1996		9,000	I	Cranswick et al. 1999		65,000 Iceland/ UK/Ireland	I	Rose & Scott 1997	
Bar-tailed Godwit	W	52,500	I	Cayford & Waters 1996		16,000	I	Way et al. 1993	16,000–20,000 = minimum	115,000 W Palearctic	I	Rose & Scott 1997	

Species/population	Season	GB population	GB population unit	GB population source	GB population derivation	All-Ireland population	All-Ireland population unit	All-Ireland population source	All-Ireland population derivation	Bio-geographic population and name	Bio-geographic population unit	Bio-geographic population source	Bio-geographic population derivation
Whimbrel	B	530	P	Dore & Ellis 1994						220,000 Europe/W Africa	P	Rose & Scott 1997	Winter figure divided by three & rounded to nearest 10,000
Whimbrel	P	5,000	I	Cranswick et al. 1997		Unknown				650,000 Europe/W Africa	I	Rose & Scott 1997	600,000–700,000 = midpoint
Whimbrel	W	<15	I	Lack 1986		<15	I	Lack 1986		650,000 Europe/W Africa	I	Rose & Scott 1997	600,000–700,000 = midpoint
Curlew	B	33,000	P	Piersma 1986	33,000–38,000 prs = minimum	12,000	P	Reed 1985		120,000 Europe	P	Rose & Scott 1997	Winter figure divided by three & rounded
Curlew	W	115,000	I	Cayford & Waters 1996		87,500	I	Cranswick et al. 1999		348,000 Europe	I	Rose & Scott 1997	
Spotted Redshank	W	120	I	Cayford & Waters 1996						75,000 Europe/W Africa	I	Rose & Scott 1997	75,000–150,000 inds = minimum
Redshank	B	30,600	P	Piersma 1986	30,600–33,600 prs = minimum	4,400	P	Gibbons et al. 1993	4,400–5,000 = minimum	59,000 Total T. t. totanus	P	Rose & Scott 1997	Winter figure divided by three / Total population of T. t. totanus
Redshank	P	120,000	I	Cranswick et al. 1997		Unknown				177,000 total T. t. totanus	I	Rose & Scott 1997	Wintering figure used / Total population of T. t. totanus
Redshank	W	114,000	I	Cayford & Waters 1996		24,500	I	Way et al. 1993		177,000 total T. t. totanus	I	Rose & Scott 1997	Total population of T. t. totanus
Greenshank	B	1,440	P	Hancock et al. 1997						57,600 Europe	P	Hagemeijer & Blair 1997	57,612–83,189 = rounded minimum
Greenshank	W	380	I	Cayford & Waters 1996		900	I	Cranswick et al. 1999		550,000 Europe/W Africa	I	Rose & Scott 1997	100,000–1,000,000 = midpoint
Wood Sandpiper	B	10	P	SNH unpublished						298,800 Europe	P	Hagemeijer & Blair 1997	298,842–412,474 = rounded minimum
Turnstone	W	64,400	I	Cayford & Waters 1996		22,500	I	Cranswick et al. 1999		67,000 Europe (wintering)	I	Rose & Scott 1997	
Red-necked Phalarope	B	36	M	Stone et al. 1997						65,500 Europe	P	Hagemeijer & Blair 1997	65,536–94,391 = rounded minimum

Species/population	Season	GB population	GB population unit	GB population source	GB population derivation	All-Ireland population	All-Ireland population unit	All-Ireland population source	All-Ireland population derivation	Bio-geographic population name	Bio-geographic population unit	Bio-geographic population source	Bio-geographic population derivation
Arctic Skua	B	3,200	P	Walsh et al. 1995	Territories equated to pairs					30,000 NE Atlantic	P	Lloyd et al. 1991	20,000–40,000 = midpoint
Great Skua	B	8,500	P	Walsh et al. 1995	Territories equated to pairs					13,600 World	P	Lloyd et al. 1991	
Mediterranean Gull	B	31	P	Ogilvie et al. 1996	31–45 pairs = minimum					184,000 Europe	P	Hagemeijer & Blair 1997	183,925–339,963 = rounded minimum
Black-headed Gull	B	167,000	P	Lloyd et al. 1991		53,800	P	Gibbons et al. 1993		1,650,000 World	P	Lloyd et al. 1991	
Black-headed Gull	W	1,900,000	I	Stone et al. 1997		1,100,000	I	Lack 1986	Difference between estimates for Britain/Ireland and GB	5,000,000 NW Europe	I	Rose & Scott 1997	Minimum
Common Gull	B	68,000	P	Lloyd et al. 1991		3,600	P	Gibbons et al. 1993		124,000 NW & C Europe/Atlantic/Mediterranean	P	Lloyd et al. 1991	
Common Gull	W	900,000	I	Stone et al. 1997		67,500	I	Lack 1986		1,600,000 NW & C Europe/Atlantic/Med.	I	Rose & Scott 1997	
Lesser Black-backed Gull	B	83,000	P	Lloyd et al. 1991		5,200	P	Gibbons et al. 1993		124,000 total L. f. graellsii	P	Lloyd et al. 1991	Total population of L. f. graellsii
Lesser Black-backed Gull	W	500,000	I	Stone et al. 1997		70,000	I	Lack 1986		400,000	I	Rose & Scott 1997	400,000–500,000 = minimum; total population of L. f. graellsii
Herring Gull	B	160,000	P	Lloyd et al. 1991		44,700	P	Gibbons et al. 1993		940,000 NW European & Iceland/W Europe	P	Lloyd et al. 1991	Includes both L. a. argentatus and L. a. argenteus
Great Black-backed Gull	B	19,000	P	Lloyd et al. 1991		4,500	P	Gibbons et al. 1993		95,546 Europe	P	Hagemeijer & Blair 1997	95,546–121,233 = minimum
Kittiwake	B	490,000	P	Lloyd et al. 1991		50,200	P	Gibbons et al. 1993		3,170,000 North Atlantic = total R. t. tridactyla	P	Lloyd et al. 1991	Calculated using mid-points of ranges presented Total population of R. t. tridactyla

Species/population	Season	GB population	GB population unit	GB population source	GB population derivation	All-Ireland population	All-Ireland population unit	All-Ireland population source	All-Ireland population derivation	Bio-geographic population and name	Bio-geographic population unit	Bio-geographic population source	Bio-geographic population derivation
Sandwich Tern	B	14,000	P	Lloyd et al. 1991		4,400	P	Gibbons et al. 1993		132,000 Europe	P	Hagemeijer & Blair 1997	
Sandwich Tern	P	42,000	I	JNCC unpublished	extrapolated from breeding population	13,200	I	Gibbons et al. 1993		396,000 Europe	I	Derived from Hagemeijer & Blair 1997	Breeding population × 3
Roseate Tern	B	64	P	Stone et al. 1997		400	P	Gibbons et al. 1993	>400 = minimum estimate	1,770 Europe	P	Lloyd et al. 1991	
Common Tern	B	12,300	P	Gibbons et al. 1993		3,100	P	Gibbons et al. 1993		195,105 Europe	P	Hagemeijer & Blair 1997	195,105–227,250 = minimum
Arctic Tern	B	44,000	P	Gibbons et al. 1993		2,500	P	Gibbons et al. 1993		900,000 Europe/North Atlantic	P	Lloyd et al. 1991	
Little Tern	B	2,400	P	Lloyd et al. 1991		390	P	Gibbons et al. 1993		20,643 Europe	P	Hagemeijer & Blair 1997	20,643–22,799 = minimum
Guillemot	B	703,500	P	Lloyd et al. 1991	67% of popn as individuals	102,510	P	Gibbons et al. 1993		2,250,000 North Atlantic	P	Lloyd et al. 1991	Conversion of 0.67 used between Apparently Occupied Sites and individual birds
Razorbill	B	99,160	P	Lloyd et al. 1991	67% of popn as individuals	22,780	P	Gibbons et al. 1993		575,000 total Alca torda islandica	P	Lloyd et al. 1991	Total population of Alca torda islandica Conversion of 0.67 used between Apparently Occupied Sites and individual birds Midpoints of national ranges used
Puffin	B	449,000	P	Lloyd et al. 1991	50% of popn as individuals	20,500	P	Gibbons et al. 1993		901,000 total Fratercula arctica grabae	P	Lloyd et al. 1991	Total population of Fratercula arctica grabae Conversion of 0.5 used between Apparently Occupied Sites and individual birds
Short-eared Owl	B	1,000	P	Gibbons et al. 1993	1,000–3,500 = minimum					13,400 Europe	P	Hagemeijer & Blair 1997	13,376–26,265 = rounded minimum
Nightjar	B	3,400	M	Morris et al. 1994						224,000 Europe	M	Hagemeijer & Blair 1997	223,921–264,419 = rounded minimum

Species/population	Season	GB population	GB population unit	GB population source	GB population derivation	All-Ireland population	All-Ireland population unit	All-Ireland population source	All-Ireland population derivation	Bio-geographic population name	Bio-geographic population unit	Bio-geographic population source	Bio-geographic population derivation
Kingfisher	B	3,300	P	Gibbons et al. 1993	3,300–5,500 = minimum	1,300	P	Gibbons et al. 1993	1,300–2,100 = minimum	47,302 Europe	P	Hagemeijer & Blair 1997	Hagemeijer 47,302–66,752 = minimum
Woodlark	B	1,500	P	Wotton & Gillings 2000						1,050,000 Europe	P	Hagemeijer & Blair 1997	Hagemeijer 1,050,376–2,239,048 = rounded minimum
Aquatic Warbler	P	67	I	EN unpublished	Count 1997					11,220 World population	I	Tucker & Heath 1994	Breeding range minimum (3,740) × 3 = 11,220 inds
Dartford Warbler	B	1,600	P	Gibbons & Wotton 1996	1,600–1,890 = minimum					2,025,000 Europe	P	Hagemeijer & Blair 1997	Hagemeijer 2,025,456–3,635,791 = rounded minimum
Chough	B	340	P	Bignal et al. 1997		906	P	Berrow et al. 1993		12,265 Europe	P	Hagemeijer & Blair 1997	Hagemeijer 12,265–17,370 = minimum
Chough	W	689	I	Bignal et al. 1997		2,633	I	Berrow et al. 1993		36,800 Europe	I	Derived from Hagemeijer & Blair 1997	Breeding range minimum (12,265) × 3 = 36,795 inds then rounded
Snow Bunting	B	70	P	Stone et al. 1997	70–100 = minimum					220,000 Europe	P	Hagemeijer & Blair 1997	Hagemeijer 223,986–634,300 prs = rounded minimum
Fair Isle Wren	B	37	M	SNH unpublished	Count 1997					37 World	M	SNH unpublished	Count 1997
Scottish Crossbill	B	300	P	Stone et al. 1997	300–1,250 = minimum					300 World	P	Stone et al. 1997	Stone et al. 300–1250 prs = minimum